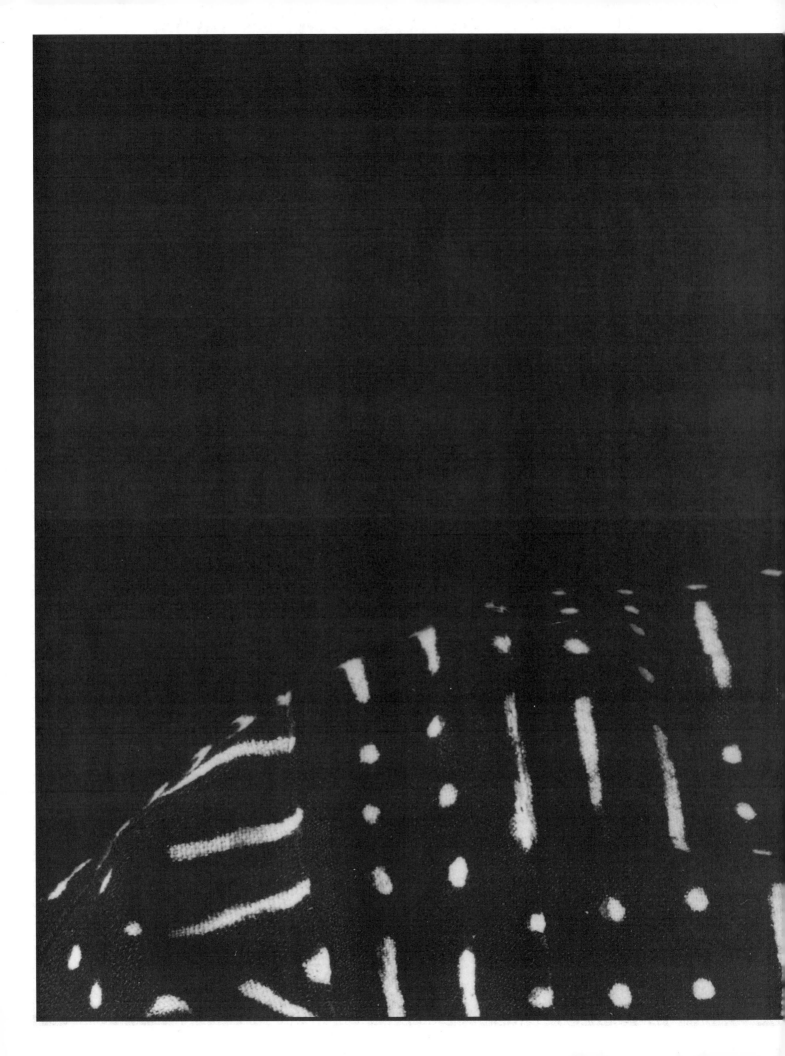

Jackie Tales

THE MAGIC OF CREATING STORIES AND THE ART OF TELLING THEM

BY JACKIE TORRENCE

INTRODUCTION BY OSSIE DAVIS
EDITED BY PETER BRADFORD
WITH PHOTOGRAPHS BY
MICHAEL PATEMAN

AVON BOOKS
NEW YORK

AVON BOOKS, INC.
1350 Avenue of the Americas
New York, New York 10019

Copyright © 1998 by Jackie Torrence
Design by Peter Bradford and Danielle Whiteson. Photographs
by Michael Pateman and Chris Cassidy. Excerpts from the
Jackie Torrence video series are used in several captions with the
kind permission of National Training Network (800) 686-1001.
ISBN: 0-380-97582-3

Visit our website at **http://WWW.AvonBooks.com**

Library of Congress Cataloging-in-Publication Data:
Torrence, Jackie.
     Jackie Tales : the magic of creating stories and the art of
 telling them / by Jackie Torrence ; introduction by Ossie Davis ;
 edited by Peter Bradford ; with photographs by Michael Pateman. —
 1st ed.
        p. cm.
     1. Storytelling. 2. Folklore—Performance. I. Title.
 GR72.3.T67   1998
 808.5'43—dc21   97-52626
                                                                      CIP

First Avon Books Printing: June 1998
AVON TRADEMARK REG. U.S. PAT. OFF. AND IN OTHER COUNTRIES,
MARCA REGISTRADA, HECHO EN U.S.A.
Printed in the U.S.A.
First Edition
QPK 10 9 8 7 6 5 4 3 2 1

CONTENTS

TO JOHN ULLMAN AND IRENE NAMKUNG

Storytelling has now been my career for 30 years, but 50 years of serious listening and learning have helped me create a special telling technique. My family members originated "the technique," I merely took my place in line and carried the family craft just a step farther. I thank God for placing me among such talented relations; whatever I received by way of birthright has provided my livelihood and subsistence. Also, all my teachers from kindergarten through college contributed to my telling technique, and I thank them for their untiring years of dedication to me and other students who were, at times, determined not to yield to education.

I also must thank the folks of Salisbury and Granite Quarry, North Carolina, for their steadfast encouragement. The "Area News" reporter for the *Salisbury Post*, Mrs. Rose Post, has been a supporter from the very first day we met. I will never forget being very nervous and almost speechless before one of my most important performances. She whispered in my ear, "*You* are one of a kind. They have come to hear *you—speak!*" Thanks Rose. And many thanks to Mr. Paul Fisher, President of F&M Bank and Belks Department Store, whose assurance has kept me working in the off-seasons, to Michael Franks of Earwig Music in Chicago, to the folks of Weston Woods Studio in Weston, Connecticut, and to my friend Jimmy Neil Smith, founder and director of the National Storytelling Association.

My special thanks to the Great Actor, Mr. Ossie Davis, whose love for stories and family tradition put him in my audience one day and made us fans of each other. I also thank Brian Enright for helping my dreams of videotaping come together at last, and August House in Little Rock for publishing the book that was my special "brain child."

My thanks to Peter Bradford for hearing *my* sound and Michael Pateman for seeing and photographing the images, and great thanks to Avon Books for understanding the book they made. And of course, I am grateful to everybody who has sat in my audience, read my books, and watched my tapes. Without you the stories cannot live.

Last, but not least, I want to thank my folks at home. My daughter Lori, my niece Ava, and my grandson Boyce serve as my constant inspiration. —*Jackie Torrence, Salisbury, 1998.*

FOREWORD

Far more than enough has been said about television and its smothering effects on our lives. For good or bad, whether it elevates us or eats us up (or both), that bright, one-eyed monster in the corner is here to stay. So, while television wages its war of mindless distraction, we best find ways to outflank the thing before it outflanks us.

Jackie Torrence thinks we are losing the war. "Something has happened to our children today. Television is a wonderful thing, but it doesn't help children talk, it doesn't ask them to create, and it doesn't ask them to imagine. They seem to have lost their imaginations."

The imagination is our best way to reach and impress children with what we want them to know. Long before television, long before books, all cultures did this with their myths, legends, and parables. Transported in stories, they taught children what was right and what wasn't, talked about love, and celebrated success, heroes, and wisdom. But, we have slowly given up those storytelling ways. We tend to take the easy route now, forego the fun and intimacy, and relegate the teaching to school and books and the you-know-what in the corner.

If only her own huge energies were called for, Jackie Torrence could likely restore the oral tradition all by herself. But she believes that stories have the power to stir the teller as well as the listener and she wants to pass that power on. "I want to make you laugh," she says. "I even want to make you cry a little. If you glean an important message from anything I say, take it. I give it freely."

This book is meant to help her do that. It was recorded and photographed in four 10-hour days at Jackie's home in Salisbury, North Carolina. It was also videotaped so that the photographs could be placed exactly where they occurred. On the book pages, her stories are typographically phrased to match her speaking rhythms, and every shriek and moan is caught as well as phonetics allow. Her explanations of the stories are placed in the page margins, and "stage directions" reflecting her gestures and expressions are within the stories. The long recording sessions must have been very tiring for her, but she laughed all the way through. More than that, I could not possibly describe the richness of the experience. —*Peter Bradford, New York, 1998.*

INTRODUCTION *By Ossie Davis*

It would be wonderful if everybody everywhere, particularly you reading this book, could spend some quality time listening to Jackie Torrence telling one of her stories. Her face—especially the eyes, keep your eye on those eyes—her hands, her voice, her body itself, pregnant with the story she is telling—all are one. I've never seen so close an identification between the art and the artist in my life. These are the things I think you can learn from Jackie:

First, read these stories aloud as soon as you can, and make sure there are children present to hear you. Don't be bashful, don't be shamefaced or halfhearted—pussyfooting around is the best way in the world to kill a story. And speak up, for heaven's sake, so they can hear you. It's not you they are listening to anyway, it's the story.

"... That's who Jackie Torrence really is, today's Griot."

Griots were the storytellers of Africa who gathered and passed on information about the tribe. They were the newspapers and media of their time.

So just be loud and clear, with Jackie's joy and enthusiasm. Go ahead. Do it, I dare you. Read this book to the young folk, Jackie will show you how. That's who Jackie Torrence really is, today's Griot. Collecting stories of her people, writing many of her own, then telling them every chance she gets. Just do what Jackie tells you and your children might wind up liking you as much as they like television. This is your chance—do it!

But if you can't find any children to listen, or worse still, if children intimidate you too much, then by all means try one or two of the stories on yourself. Go right ahead, get in front of the mirror and ham it up, make a fool of yourself. Nobody's watching but

Jackie and me, and I swear to you, we will never tell anybody.

You see, as Jackie says, and as Zora Neale Hurston said before her, the worst thing you can do to a story is just leave it there, leave it lying flat and helpless on the page all by itself, alone and unattended. A story is a living, breathing thing, and it requires, if not love, at least some of your personal attention, like any other pet that you might have. You can't leave the care and feeding of stories to Jackie alone. You've got to pitch in too, and pay attention! Or the stories will die. And according to Zora, if our stories die, we will die. All our stories need a good telling now and then to keep them firm and healthy. Jackie is talking all over the place, trying to keep them alive—the woman never stops—but she can't do it alone. She needs help from you!

Okay, Okay, so you have a voice that gives even you the hives. Well then, in silence if you must keep your mouth shut, there's still a feast for you here—a book full of goodies that will live on even if

"Just do what Jackie tells you . . ."

everybody else besides Jackie decides to run and hide. You don't have to mouth the words or mumble as you go—just read them. All alone by yourself, uttering nary a sound. These little black and white words will speak for themselves, taking you back to a world that belongs to your childhood. A world you must never forget. And neither must your children.

All right. That's enough talking to you. Who's next?

Ossie Davis is one of America's most prolific performing artists. His Broadway plays include A Raisin in the Sun *and his own satirical farce,* Purlie Victorious; *his films include* Grumpy Old Men *and* The Client. *He published his first novel* Just Like Martin *and is now writing a joint biography with his wife Ruby Dee.*

MY TALE   By Jackie Torrence

I was just a little girl when I was taken in by Grandma and Grandpa, because my mother lived in Chicago and I couldn't be with her. They lived in Second Creek in North Carolina, just a little way from where I live today, and I spent six years of my childhood there. It was a wonderful time for me. But I was all by myself out there, alone with two old folks who didn't know what in the world to do with this little girl.

And you know, I was born with a speech impediment. I had impacted teeth, so I couldn't talk real good. Grandpa would always caution folks, "Don't answer yes to anything she says 'cause you don't know what she's saying." So everybody would just say, "Hah?" when I'd ask them something. But I talked all the time anyway, I talked day and night. We'd go for a walk and I'd say, "Granddaddy, what's that?" He'd say, "That's a tree." "Granddaddy, what's that?" He'd say, "That's a rock." "What's that, Granddaddy?" And he'd say, "That's another tree." Then, when he got tired of me just talking and talking and talking, he'd say, "Wait a minute. *Listen*." I'd say, "What are we listening for?" He'd say, "Well, I ain't gonna be able to hear it if you keep running your mouth." Then they'd put me in bed at six o'clock when they finally had enough of me.

When you hear me tell my stories today, what you see and hear is a little girl who played by herself for years. Even after my grandpa died and my aunt Mildred took me in, nobody played with me because my aunt didn't like other children in the house. So I played alone. I told stories out loud, and I practiced voice all the time, making gestures and all, because I made believe I was on television.

But what I really wanted to be was a dancer. I used to leap across the floor on my toes, Bam! Bam! Bam! My aunt Mildred would say, *"You know, they don't make tutus for elephants."* Oh, she was something, my aunt was; she kept after me all the time about one thing or another. So I danced with my hands. I'd sit in front of the mirror on Sunday afternoon and I'd watch ballet on that program *Omnibus*. They would make those moves and I would make them with my hands, you know; that's about as far as I could rise off the floor. Oh, it was wonderful, I just *loved* to do that.

"They lived in Second Creek . . ."

Now, my full name is Jacqueline LaVonia Carson Seals Torrence, and I tell you, that third name is loaded, that Carson has a lot of history packed into it. My great-grandfather was a slave named Samuel Mitchell Carson. He was a teacher and a minister and a real smart man. Even when I was very young I learned about the people in my family, and I knew how highly respected they were. I never had to wonder about my identity, I always knew who I was.

But I still had that speech impediment. It just engulfed my life. In school, when I'd open my mouth to speak, everybody in the class would tuck their heads down on their desks and laugh. Well, that really hurt my feelings. If they weren't laughing at what I said, they laughed because I was fat and pigeon-toed and couldn't run without falling flat on my face. Many a day I'd go home with dry tracks of tears streaking down my face. My dear aunt would say, "What have you been crying about?" "They said I was fat." She'd just get so angry. "You sure are silly. If they say that to you every day, then you oughtta believe it."

Then in fifth grade, I had a teacher named Miss Pauline Pharr. She was kind, sweet, just out of college, and she loved her class. Well, we *were* all exceptionally lovable children, you know. Miss Pharr gave us an assignment. "We've got two weeks before Halloween," she said. "I want everybody to be creative and write a good scary story. Then everybody will read their story to the class." And I

". . . I thought, 'Oh boy, I'm dead.'"

thought, "Oh boy, I'm dead. I can write the story, but I'm gonna have a hard time reading it." Well, I'm sitting there fighting back the tears, then they started leaking down my face, then I started with the jerks.

But sitting right next to me was James, the class tattletale. He was watching me. He told everything. He decided to tell. His hand went up, then his other hand went up. "Ooh! Ooh! Ooh! Miss Pauline Pharr! Miss Pharr! Miss Pauline! Miss Pauline Pharr!" And he pointed at me. "She ain't writing." Miss Pharr saw that I was crying, so she came over and bent real low. "What's wrong?" And I told her. Everybody was laughing. But Miss Pharr said, "Don't pay them any mind. I tell you what. If you write a good story, cross all your *t*'s and dot your *i*'s, put all the commas in and spell every word right, I'll read that story for you. That'll fix 'em." And I said, "Okay."

I went about writing it, and let me tell you, I double-checked every word to make sure it was spelled right. Every *t* was crossed and I made little circles at the top of the *i*'s just to make sure they had a dot on them. I wrote about Mr. Henry and a mule named Ned on a scary road on Halloween night (see page 192). Miss Pharr thought it was wonderful. She read it and gave me two great big red check marks. I didn't have to cry that day 'cause she patted me and said, "You did real good." And I thought, "You did too." I really believe my healing began with that story.

And then in the ninth grade I found my favorite teacher, Abna Aggrey Lancaster. She worked with me night and day on the way I talked, she helped me in school and she helped me in life. I was ashamed to stand in front of people, you know. I wanted to hide the fact that I was fat. If I had to stand onstage, I couldn't hide *anything*. But Miss Lancaster said, "No, darling, that's all right. The way we get by that is with the hair. You have *lovely* hair." She said, "Fix your hair, fix your face, and wear very nice clothes." I said, "But how can I hide my fat?" She said, "You don't hide it, you feel good about it. You're not the slimmest thing in the world, we know we're fat, so why get upset about it? If we work on the hair, nobody will see anything else." Miss Lancaster said, "Are you going to succumb to what a few people think? And miss out on life? No? Well, let's get on with it then."

That's what she helped me understand, that everybody can find their own place of happiness. Yes, you are born in this world to carry a burden, everybody has a burden, but carry it proudly, 'cause if you look over there, somebody's got one much bigger than yours. For years I was told I was going to be happy when I lost weight. I never lost weight. I tried my best to be slender two or three times and I nearly killed myself. Then, when I couldn't walk so well and I landed in that wheelchair, I wanted to die. I like to walk out on a stage, you know, I like to swing my dress out when I sit down like my aunt Sally. But now I can't do that. So I thought, "For some reason, God put me in this wheelchair; here again is my burden, so I'll deal with it." I've decided to be happy. I think, "Shoot, this is great. Like Grandma said, 'You gotta make yourself bloom where you're planted.'"

"I think, 'Shoot, this is great.'"

I told my first story when I was a reference librarian in High Point, North Carolina. It snowed one day and the librarian didn't show up, but all the kids did. "Read them a book or show them a film or something," I was told. Well, I told them a mountain tale and they loved it. "Tell it again, tell it again," they said, and I did. And that's how all of this started.

Jump Tales

JUMP TALES

Over the years, I have loved telling these scary little stories. I call them Jump Tales. At the end of the tale there's always a *"BOO!"* or something that causes the child to jump. I love that and they love it too. It's a special kind of story and it takes a lot of care and hard work. You won't get a good *"BOO!"* just because it's at the end; you don't have success unless you work toward that success. You must set the story up carefully and take your time doing it.

The Danish people were famous for their Jump Tales, and there are very old and wonderful English Jump Tales too. The English have a peculiar way about them, and their Jump Tales are really interesting and sometimes very subtle. For instance, the one about Michael and Mary called *The Yellow Ribbon*. There's such a long buildup and it's

". . . there's always a 'BOO!' . . ."

so simple. It seems to be a very quiet story, you know. The kids think *"Aaaaaahhhhh,"* and they relax right up to the end, and then they really jump. That's English, that's quite English.

All these stories were ways to keep children entertained in the old days and they still are, especially if you say to them before you begin, "This is a *scary story.*" They will sit there waiting for the scary part to come. Then you come to the *"BOO!"* at the end and that's it. *Ooohhhh*, that's when the goose bumps rise, oh, they really love to be frightened. And I love to frighten them too.

But when you tell a Jump Tale, remember that the expressions in your face and your gestures are what children watch, but your whole body is telling the story. You must put all of yourself into it.

People often ask about the difference in telling stories to adults and children. I say that when you tell stories to children you have to be more detailed. "What do you mean?" they ask. Well, because children don't have worldly experience, they don't really understand abstract terms, like "*The king was wicked.*" That's all I have to say to adults. But if I say, "The king was wicked" to children, they say, "Wicked? How wicked was he?" What child knows the word "wicked" or understands it? So I have to say, "*The king was wicked. He was so wicked he kicked his dog, he stepped on his cat's tail, and he pinched his mama.*" That's really wicked and they understand that. They love that. So you add some good expressions too. As you show the king sneaking up on his mama and pinching her, "*Erk! Erk! Erk!*" you make a face; don't be afraid to make a face.

You must remember that children today are very sophisticated. They watch television, animated films and film strips in school, and

". . . don't be afraid to make a face."

they see a lot of expressive characters. The actors and the people who perform for them do everything it takes to make them feel and understand emotions. A lot of things that you speak about, like love and hate, that's all abstract. Children don't have the experience to really understand those feelings. So you must show them in your face. You have to make big expressions, you have to use big gestures. That's what's good about telling stories, you can make those faces. I love to read stories to children. But telling them, as my daughter used to say, "from your mouth" is easier, because you can watch the children's eyes. *You* become the character, *you* become the story, and they lose themselves completely in what you're saying.

THE BIG HAIRY TOE

Now, this is the story of *The Big Hairy Toe*. Once upon a time, there lived a man just down the road a piece. He was a very, very *nice* man. He lived in a nice little cabin, and he kept it very clean and neat. But he was very poor.

In fact, this man was so poor he couldn't shop in the grocery store. He had to pick his berries and his greens and his fruit from the woods. Why, you might see him any time with his basket, picking berries and nuts and greens.

Well, this time the man was in the woods with his basket, picking berries from a bush. The best berries were on the bottom of the bush, so there he picked and filled his basket with the *(stretch word way out)* *juuuuuuuuuuiciest* berries.

When all at once, as he leaned into the bush, picking the *biiiggest* and the *juuuuuuuiciest* berries, he touched something. *(frown)*

"Oh," he said. "That does not feel familiar." And he pulled whatever it was from the bush.

"*Ooooh*. What is *that?* *(pick it up, squint, look closely)* It looks like a Big . . . Hairy . . . *Toe. Hmmmm.* *(frown)* I never saw a toe that wasn't connected to a foot. I never had a toe that wasn't connected to *my* foot. Well now, I think I'll take it home."

And he dropped the Big Hairy Toe in his basket. He continued to pick berries, and when he finished, he went home.

At home, when he turned his basket of berries
in to a great bucket of water to wash them,
what should pop up to the top but *the Toe.*

"*Ooooh*," he said.

"*Yeeewwwww*," he said. *(squinch eyes)*

"What shall I do with the Hairy Toe? Oh, I know,
I shall place it on the mantelpiece." *(raise it and place it high)*
Then he washed the berries and put them in a bowl.

"Ummm," he said.

He was hungry.

So he settled down before the fire and he ate
the berries . . . as he watched the Toe. *(eat the berries, look up)*

"Never seen *(cackle, cackle)* a toe like that before."
And he ate all the berries he could hold.

He was very tired from his long day in the woods.

"Ah," he said. *(yawn, stretch)* "I think I will go to bed."

And he blew out the candles in the cabin,
went to his room and removed his clothes,
put on his nightshirt and pulled the covers back,
blew out the candle in his room, *(blow quickly on finger)*
pulled himself into bed and the covers over his face.

"*Aaaaaaaah*." His head dropped upon the pillow,
and he fell off to sleep. *(snore and snore and snore)*

But over in the night, as he slept, he realized
that he had eaten too many berries.

"Oh," he said. *(squint in pain)* "I have this awful pain
in my tummy. *Ooo*, I've just eaten too many berries.
I must take some medicine."

So he got up, and he walked across the room,
and he opened the bedroom door.

"*Ooooh*," he said, "I must have some medicine."

But as he opened the bedroom door,

*". . . and he ate the berries . . .
as he watched the Toe."*

Then the man takes the Big Toe
home. Good heavens, something
that strange you'd take home?
Why, you would say, "Oh no, I
wouldn't take that thing home."
But this man takes it home just
the same. Now he's setting
himself up, building the story
triangle even higher. He brings
the Toe into the house and puts it
on the mantelpiece, of all places.
Now, this is the part I really like.
As the character eats the berries,
I can see that the listener has
forgotten about me and is now
thinking like the character.

"Oh, I have this awful pain . . ."

Now, all children know what
happens when you eat too much
ice cream, when you eat too
many plums, or when you eat too
many grapes. Your tummy is
going to ache. Now, this man's
stomach aches in the night, so he
must get up. And it's daaark.

he heard something near the fireplace.

It was a *voice*.

And the voice whispered, *(far away and very quietly)* "*Wheeeeere's . . . Myyyyyy . . . Haaaaairy . . . Toe?*"

"*Oooooo*," said the man. *(eyes wide)* "What was *that?* Mmm, it's my imagination. *Oooowwww*, *(hold your tummy)* my tummy hurts. I must have my medicine. That voice *must* be my imagination. Let me be sure."

So he listened again.

This time the voice was closer and louder. *(louder)* "*WHEeeeere's . . . MYyyyyy . . . HAAaaairy . . . TOE?*"

"*Oh*," said the man. "That's not my imagination. Somebody just said, *(very fast)* *Where'smyhairytoe?*"

He quickly stepped back into the bedroom, slammed the door, and stood there.

"What must I *do?*" he said. *(eyes very wide)*

"*Oooooo . . . What was that?*"

He opens the door and he hears the whisper. Uh oh. There's something in there looking for its Toe. Now, that's really strange. Something has removed its Toe and now it's coming back to look for it? Oh my goodness, children love that, they think that's just wonderful. The story triangle is getting higher. This is the part I like the most, when the creature first appears. When the voice is heard again, it's much louder. Suddenly the child has become the story's character—the child is the one who's frightened.

"There's something strange in my house," he said.

"I know, I will hide."

He looked all around the room, *(rushed and frantic)* but there was only one place.

A closet.

He quickly ran to the closet and opened the door, stepped inside and grabbed the key, and placed it in the lock. Click, click, *click.*

"*Heh heh*, I'm safe. *Hah, haaaaaaah.*"

But inside the closet, *(whisper, eyes wide, lean forward)* it was . . . dark . . . daaaaark . . . *daaaaaaaaaaaaaaaark.*

Then, all of a sudden, the door that this man had locked himself was *opening.*

Squuueeeeeeeee*eeeeeeeeeeeeeeeeeeeeeeek.*

And coming across the floor *(voice rising)* he could hear that Voice. *(much louder)*

"*WHOOO'S . . . GOT . . . MY . . . HAIRY . . . TOE?*

"**YOOOOOU!!!** *(loud scream and reach out grabbing)*

"**YOOO***OOU'VE GOT MY HAIRY TOE!*"

"*Ooooooooo*," said the man. *(frightened, with wide eyes)*

"But I don't, *(shaking) I don't.*

It's on the mantelpiece, *(pointing) it's on the mantelpiece.*"

And quickly, *(very fast)*
the monster turned the man aloose,
ran to the mantelpiece,
grabbed the Toe,
ran off into the night,
and disappeared.

And nobody's ever seen that monster or that great Big Hairy Toe again.

. . . And *that's* the end of that.

"I know, I will hide."

▬▬▬▬▬▬▬▬▬▬

What do you do when there's something after you? You hide. And where is the best place to hide? In a closet with a door you can lock. But what can unlock the door? The same thing that can remove its toe from its foot and lose it. The door is unlocked, and it opens. By now the child thinks, "I'm in big trouble." He's near the top of the story triangle.

"YOOOOOU'VE GOT MY . . ."

▬▬▬▬▬▬▬▬▬▬

The story is now at its pinnacle, the big, big jump at the top of the triangle. The story's over. Now, how do you settle that child down? The monster drops the man, grabs his Hairy Toe, runs off, and disappears in the night. Nobody's ever seen him since. The scary thing is gone, the danger's gone, the child laughs.

Michael and Mary had known each other all their lives. When they were babies they would play together in a sandbox, and little Michael would crawl over to Mary, who was building her little sand house with her little shovel, and he would say in baby talk, you know, in his cutest little voice, "Mary, whatcha doing?"

And she'd say, *(grumpy face)* "Hmmm."

And he'd say, "You look pretty."

Well, I'm not sure if that's *really* what he said, but then I think he said, "Mary, *(lean forward)* why do you have a yellow ribbon around your neck?"

And she said in baby talk, "Heee*heee, go away.*"

Well, soon they were together in the first grade in school. When Mary was swinging and swinging, Michael just sort of stood and watched her.

He said, "Can I push you?" *(push your hands forward)*

And she said, *(happily)* "Yes."

And he pushed her about four or five times and got the swing going *(raise hands high)* *high up* into the sky.

Suddenly he stopped her.

He said, "Can I ask you a question?"

She said, *(nod and nod)* "Uh huh."

And he said, "Tell me, Mary, *(lean forward)* why do you have that yellow ribbon around your neck?"

And she said, "Ha*haaaa*, none of your business. *Hmmm.*" *(giggle)* And she went on swinging.

Well, then they were in high school together, and they were in the library reading.

"Mary, whatcha doing?"

LEARNING TO TELL STORIES: *This is a nice little Jump Tale from England, and I will use it to explain how you can start telling stories. First, you must find a story you like, a story you really want to tell. Good stories are all around you; you can find them in the library, you hear them from your parents or from the old man down the road. You just have to keep your eyes and ears open.*

Then you must read that story five times. Don't memorize it, never memorize a story word for word. The first time you read it, make sure it will fit your listeners, and especially make sure it fits you. Don't ever tell a story you don't like. Believe it or not, if you really want to tell your story, you can be sure that children will feel that and they will really listen.

When you are sure you want to tell the story, make three copies of it. Put the first copy away to keep safe, and use the second copy as a working copy for your notes and changes. Later you can use the third copy to make a record of the story you create.

Michael walked over to Mary and said,
  "Gosh, you look so pretty today."
  And she said, *(shy and coy)* "Thank you."
  "Can I sit and look at that magazine with you?"
  "Oh," she said, "sure, *(motion forward)* come on."
  So they looked at the magazine together, then
he turned to her and said, "Got a question for ya."
  She said, *(sweetly)* "Yes, what is it?"
  He said, "Mary, tell me, why do you always wear
that yellow ribbon *(hands to your neck)* around your neck?"
  She said, *(sort of huffy)* *"None of your business."* *(look away)*
  Well then, on the night of graduation they were
standing in line in cap and gown. Michael looked
so handsome and Mary looked so beautiful.
  When they were marching together, Michael said,
"Just think, Mary, we've been in school together

". . . why do you always wear . . ."

---

*The second time you read a story,
read it for pictures. Michael and
Mary are sweet little children, but
Mary has this strange thing . . .
These are "pictures" you should
create for your listeners so that
they can see the characters and
scenes clearly. Visualize your
characters and don't be afraid to
give them personalities. You can
make notes and drawings of your
pictures on your working copy.*

for 12 years. Will I ever see you again?"

"Oh," she said, "don't be silly, you know that we are both going to the same college."

"I know, I'm so glad. But tell me something . . ."
She said, "Yes? What?"

"Why," he said, *(impatiently)* "*why* do you always wear that yellow ribbon around your neck?"

"Oh," she said. "Silly! *It's none of your business*."

Four years of college they spent together. In the very *last* year, Michael got up enough courage to say to Mary, "I have loved you from the very first time I saw you in the sandbox. Will you marry me?"

And she said, *(lovingly)* "And I have loved you too."
She smiled and said, "Yes."

"Then," he said, "can I ask you a question?"
She said, "Why, indeed. Yes."

"'Oh,' she said. 'Silly!'"

The third time you read a story, decide where you want to hem and tuck it. Adjust the words to make Mary and Michael feel right and comfortable. Remember, children are very sophisticated now, but still, some images and words in a wonderful story might be too confusing or obsolete.

And he said, "Mary, *(kind of fast)* why do you *always* wear that yellow ribbon around your neck?"

She said, "I'll tell you after we're married."

And he said, *(resigned)* "All right."

On the day of the wedding, Michael stood at the altar and turned as the bride started down the isle.

Oh, she was *breathtaking!*

She was a vision in white.

And as she approached, Michael whispered, "I love you. You are *so* beautiful. But tell me, *why* is that yellow ribbon tied around your neck?"

She said, *(whispering)* "*Shhhh. I'll tell you later.*"

Well, they were married.

They had children. Their children grew up, and their children had children. They were grandparents.

Then they were *great*-grandparents.

Soon they were very, very old.

But they still loved each other.

And one day, when they were sitting together in their rocking chairs on the porch holding hands, Michael turned slowly to Mary and said, *(quivering)*

"We've had a good life, do you realize that?"

"Oh yes," she said, "we've had a very good life."

Michael said, "I can't even count the hours and the days and the months and the years that we have been together. But they have all been sweet."

He said, "You have been a wonderful wife."

"And you a dear, *sweet* husband."

He said, "My dear, we don't have long to live. We don't have much life left. You must, you *must* help me now. Please, *please* answer my question."

And she said, "What is it, my darling?"

"...you MUST help me now."

The fourth time you read the story, put your words and your pictures together. Make sure that the story of Michael and Mary is building to the top of that story triangle I described earlier, make sure that your listeners can really see what's happening so that they will be deeply involved.

Now make a record of all your changes on the third copy. The story is yours now, so you will want to remember everything.

Maybe right away, or maybe ten years later, read the story a fifth time. You might find something you missed. You see, there is a wisdom that comes to knowing a story after reading it or telling it many times. You begin to see the characters differently, you tell it differently. Make sure you add that wisdom to the copy of the story you have put away to keep.

Now you are ready to tell it...

"Would you *please* tell me? Why have you *always* worn that yellow ribbon around your neck?"

"Oh, my dear sweet husband, I do love you. And we have been together *(shaking)* for so, *so* long.

"I know that we don't have much life left.

"I'll do better than tell you why I wear this ribbon, I'll *show* you why I wear this yellow ribbon."

And Mary's hands, *(raise trembling hands slowly to neck)* though they were very old and shook quite a bit, pulled the strings of the yellow ribbon one by one *(slow and shaking)* and as she pulled the ribbon . . . *(lunge forward and grab)* *AWWWWWWK!!!!!* *Her HEAD FELL OFF!!!!!*

. . . And *that's* the end of that.

"... as she pulled the ribbon ..."

The first time I recorded this story, I was in a little booth with the recording man. He was tilted back on his chair, and when I got to the end, he jumped way up and back against a filing cabinet. There was blood everywhere, and he had to have 36 stitches on his head. He just jumped back and Bam! Boy, I really felt bad.

THE RING

THOSE UNIVERSAL TRUTHS:
When you create or pick a story to tell, remember the universal truths, the truths that everyone knows, like love, hate, and fear. The story of Abigail and Melissa is about love and jealousy in the family, something we all know. Sometimes we can't explain such things, so we make up stories for them. Once a child said, "Beauty is skin-deep, and ugly is to the bone? What does that mean?" I said, "Well, it's hard to explain, so let me tell you this story."

High up in the mountains, in a little town called Hudson in North Carolina, there lived two little girls. They were sisters, but one was a year older than the other, and, well, the oldest girl stood about two inches taller. But they were the same size in clothes and shoes.

One was Melissa.

Melissa was the oldest, and Abigail was the baby.

They were beautiful children. Beautiful little girls with long pigtails and nice rosy red cheeks.

But Melissa *(pause)* had problems.

Melissa was kind of jealous.

She was always angry about something, and she mistreated her little sister. So what beauty she had was changing all the time.

Every time she did some evil little thing, or said something ugly to Abigail . . . she *changed*.

Beauty Is Skin-Deep . . . *Ugly Is to the Bone.*

When she was tiny, Abigail grew out of her shoes. They were just too small, she needed new ones. So her mother and father went out and they bought a pair of new little shoes, the kind that babies wear, you know, high-topped white shoes that you lace up.

Well, Melissa got mad.

Melissa said, *(grumpy and petulant)* "*I'm* the oldest. *I'm* supposed to get the new shoes first."

But Abigail said, in her tiny voice, "You can wear my shoes, you can wear them anytime you want."

But Melissa said, "No, I don't want to wear your old shoes, your old shoes *stink*."
Beauty Is Skin-Deep . . . *Ugly Is to the Bone.*

One day in elementary school, Abigail wore her favorite yellow dress to school. Her mother had made the dress. Well, they had a painting class in art and Abigail decided to paint a red house.

She had a great *big* (arms wide) jar of red paint.

She took that paint and (with big sweeping gestures) slapped it down on the paper. But when she did, she slapped red paint all up the front of her, on her face, on her arms, and on the paper too.

Oh! She *ruined* her beautiful yellow dress. The teacher washed it, but the spots were still there.

Abigail went home and her mother washed and

washed it, even bleached the dress. Just *ruined* it.

Well, Abigail cried and she cried and she *cried!*

But her mother said, "Don't you cry, dear, Mommy made that dress. I'll make another dress."

And she did.

Melissa said, "*Wait* a minute! *(angry)* *I'm* the oldest! *I'm* supposed to get a dress *(whining)* before she does! Why is *she* *(sneering)* always getting stuff?"

Abigail said, "Don't worry, Melissa, you can wear my dress if you want. It's new, you can wear it first."

Melissa said, "I don't *want* your dress, it's *ugly*."

That's the way Melissa was.

Beauty Is Skin-Deep . . . *Ugly Is to the Bone.*

Then in high school, the principal announced that the county was getting new books, but they had to last, they were going to be used for several years. He wanted everybody to protect the new books, and each child was to purchase book covers.

Now, the two sisters had about the same classes, so all of their book covers would be the same. Abigail was given pink book covers and Melissa chose the blue ones. Then she saw Abigail's covers, and decided that she liked the pink ones instead.

"*Hey, wait!*" she said. "I didn't see the pink ones. I'm supposed to have my choice. *(sulking)* *I'm* the oldest, *I'm* supposed to get what I want."

But Abigail said, "You can have my pink covers, it's all right. I don't care, they're the same size."

"I don't want them, you *touched* them."

That's the way Melissa was.

Beauty Is Skin-Deep *haha* . . . *Ugly Is to the Bone.*

And Melissa was beginning to look real ugly.

People were beginning to see how mean she was, and how stingy, and how ugly she was to her sister.

Just mistreated that poor girl all the time.

But soon they were grown-up and out of school, and they found jobs, working in the same plant. Made some kind of dresses or robes or something, and they had been working there for about a year.

Well, one night they came home for supper. Abigail was a little excited about something, so when the food was served she said,

"I can't wait any longer, I have to tell it now!

"*Oooooh!* (eyes wide and happy) I'm engaged!" she said.

"I'm going to be *married*." And she showed her beautiful diamond engagement ring. (point to your finger)

Well.

"OOOOOH! I'm engaged!"

We all know about jealousy, it's one of those truths we all have to watch out for. It's happened in my own family and in every family I know. Parents can create it by favoring one child over the other. Jealousy is a real good thing to tell stories about 'cause you can bet that most kids have heard somebody say, "Why can't you be like your sister or your brother?" You just can't grow up in a family without knowing about jealousy.

Melissa said, *(very angry)* "*Wait a minute!*

"You can't get married!" she said.

"*I'm* the oldest, *I* have to get married first.
You have to wait. You can't get married before I do.
I'm supposed to wear that diamond ring.

"*You can't do that,*" Melissa said.

Abigail said, *(laugh)* "Ha*haaah . . . bad luck, honey.*"

Well, sir, that Melissa was real angry about that.

Everybody prepared for Abigail's wedding.
Everybody had a real good time, making the dress,
making preparations. Oh! It was wonderful.

But Melissa sat in the corner, talking to herself.
"Abigail *mumble . . . mumble . . .* Abigail *mumble . . .
mumble garuumble . . . mumble mumble . . . (cross arms)
mumble mumble . . .* Abigail *garuumble mumble . . .*"

Nobody paid her any attention.

"Abigail garuumble mumble . . ."

---

*There are some powerful stories
about pride and jealousy; both of
them are big motivators. Abigail
can't show the ring without her
"Haahee." By now she knows
Melissa. "Bad luck, honey," she
says, and Melissa thinks, "Grrrrr."*

About this time she was *baaaaad* ugly.

But then, one month before her wedding, Abigail came down with something called diphtheria.

That poor girl was *so* sick, *(in a soft voice)* she *died*. The night before they buried her, they laid her out in a beautiful coffin in her wedding gown. Melissa, watching to see if anybody was looking, tiptoed slowly toward the coffin. She looked around again.

Then she took Abigail's hand, removed the ring from her finger, and placed it in her pocket.

"Hahaha*haaaaaaa*. *(sly smile)* I *told* you," she said.

"I told you I should marry first.

"I *told* you I should wear this diamond ring."

And they buried Abigail the next day.

Weeks and weeks went by. One night the family went to bed early. Melissa had waited for a chance.

". . . she was BAAAAAD ugly."

Acting ugly can make you ugly. Definitely, I have seen it happen; everybody has seen it happen. Jealousy is the worst, jealousy changes you more than anything because you can't hide it after a while. And jealousy is dangerous because it can really twist your features, it can just eat you up.

She lit two candles, brought them down the stairs, and placed them on the table. Then *(look left, look right)* she looked around to see if anybody saw her.

From her pocket she took out the diamond ring. She said to herself, "Hah*hah*. I've got the ring! Ooo*ha!* I *told* you I should wear the diamond ring."

But as she was admiring the diamond ring, a great gust of wind came right down the chimney . . .

Phhoooo! Blew the candles out.

"Myyyyyy!" said Melissa. "The wind blows a little strange tonight. I'll light the candles again." She reached over to the broom beside the fireplace and broke off a nice . . . long . . . straw.

As she leaned over the fire to light the straw, she heard something *waaaaay* up inside the chimney.

It was a *Voice.*

And the Voice said, *(very quiet and distant)*

"Wheeeeeere's myyyyyyyyyyyyyy diamond ring?"

Melissa said, *"Ooooh,* the wind blows strangely. It must be my imagination, it *couldn't* be anyone saying that, it *has* to be the wind blowing.

"I must light these candles again," she said. She broke off another straw. This time it was short, and she had to lean way into the fire to light it.

Suddenly the Voice was just above her head.

"WHEEERE'S MYYYYY DIAMOND RING?"

"Ooooooooooh!" she said. *(desperate)* "That *is* a Voice. That's not my imagination. I must get out of here. I must *hide.* I will not let it take my diamond ring."

She pulled off the ring, put it in her pocket, and looked around. There was only one place to hide.

A closet.

So she ran quickly to the closet, lifted the key, stepped inside, and locked the door.

Click, click, *click*. "Ha*haaaaa!* I'm *safe*."

But inside the closet, it was dark, dark, *daaaaark*.

And all at once, the door that she herself had locked started to open (stretch words out) all . . . by . . . *itself*.

***Skkkkrreeee*eeeeeeeeeeeeeeeeee*eeeeeeekkkkkk*.**

And across the floor, she heard the Voice,

"WHOO'S GOT MY DIA . . . (jump forward and grab)

"YOOOOOOOO*OU'VE got my diamond ring!"*

And the ghost of her sister grabbed that pocket, snatched the diamond ring, ran back,

flew up into the chimney, and disappeared.

And nobody's ever seen that ring or ghost again.

. . . And *that's* the end of that.

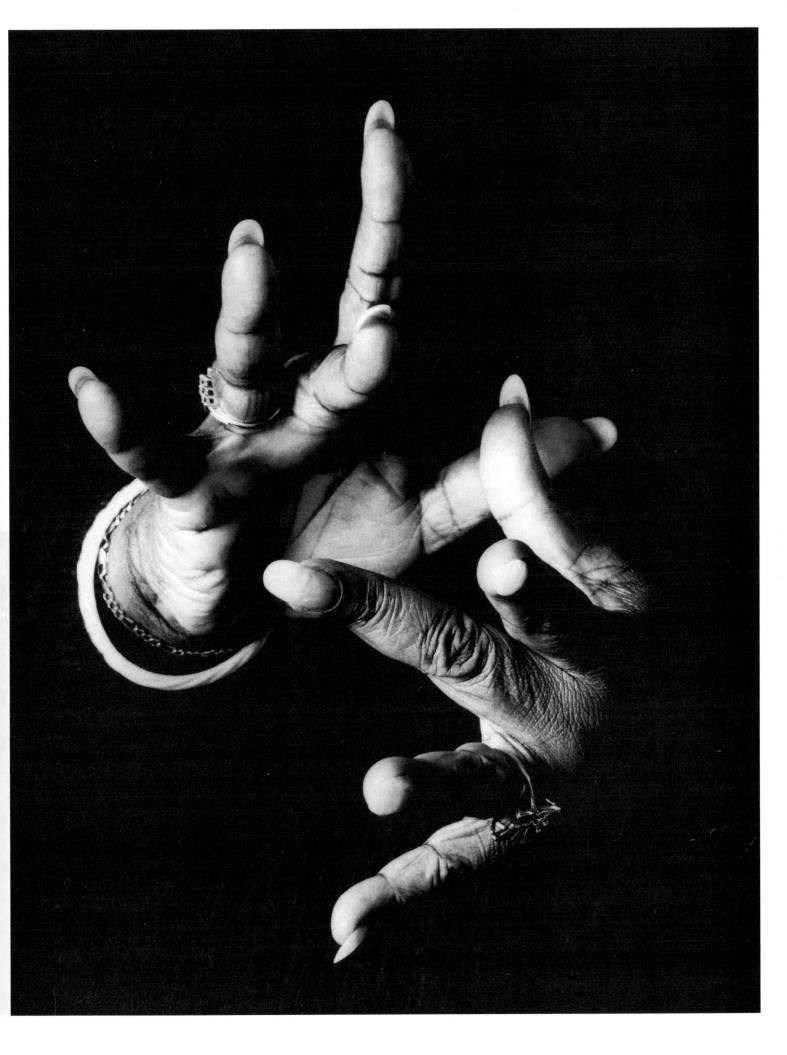

Jack Tales

JACK TALES

This is an important place for me for a simple reason: black people don't often tell Jack tales. In the early years of my career, I heard about that a lot. "What are you doing telling those Jack tales?" people would say. "What makes you think you can tell Jack tales?" Well, when I was growing up in Salisbury, North Carolina, I went to the Monroe Street School, and we had a librarian, Mrs. Corinne Thomas. Mrs. Thomas helped us learn where to find books in the library, where to find information and such things as that. But also, once a month, she took time to read to her elementary school children. Now, she often read from one special book which she kept in a little sack that she carried all the time. She would pull that book out, turn to the page she wanted, and say, "This is the story I'm going to read today." We would get all excited because we recognized the book. I didn't know it at the time, but I know now that the book she read was called *Jack Tales*, and it was by Richard Chase.

Mrs. Thomas would hold that book up, and she would read us those stories, and we thought Jack was a black child. We thought that Jack's father and Jack's mother and Jack's brothers were all black. Mrs. Corinne Thomas read that into them. And so, when I decided to tell stories myself, I knew that the Jack tales would be the first stories I would tell. Little did I know that these stories were supposedly "white" tales, as they call them. Now, the first one that I remember telling was the hardest one of all, they say, and it was one that was called *Soldier Jack*. It's the very last one in the book *Jack Tales*, and it's the one I found most fascinating because so much happens in it. Well, I'll let you be the judge of that.

You know, there was a time, just entering the first grade, when I didn't know any fairy tales at all. My aunt Mildred, who had taken me in after my granddaddy died, was a person who did not believe in make-believe. She believed in being secure. She always told me that I was going to be a teacher and she told me that I would marry a preacher. "There always has to be somebody to teach, to help people learn things," she said, "and there will always be weddings and funerals. The two of you will never be out of a job." And so, that's what I set out to do in my life. I knew if I became a teacher, I'd never be out of a job, and if I married a preacher, I'd always be secure. I was an obedient child, so I did exactly what my aunt Mildred told me.

Well, this was the woman I ran home to after my first grade teacher had read *Snow White and the Seven Dwarfs*. After hearing about Br'er Rabbit all my life, after hearing all about the slaves, I didn't know any cutesy fairy stories like Snow White. I jumped all around and I said, "You've got to hear me tell this story, *I've got to tell you this story*." I went into this long monologue about Snow White and the Seven Dwarfs. She stood there and she listened to me, and when I was through she said, "*Well, Snow White you ain't never going to be*." And she left me there in my six-year-old world trying to figure out what she meant.

Day in and day out I would come home with another fairy tale. *Cinderella?* Hah. She'd say the same thing. Now, I can look in the mirror and know I'm not going to be white, but what she really was

". . . I've got to tell you this story."

saying was that there will never, *never* be a prince on a beautiful white horse who will ride off with me into the sunset. I would have to find my own security. Teach and marry a preacher, that was the way it had to be. A doctor or a lawyer, they were way out of my realm, they would never want me, but a preacher I could get. Don't set your mind too high, you know, 'cause you can get your feelings hurt.

So all that changed my idea about fairy tales. But then during my career I would find a story like *Jack and Hardy Hardhead*, and I would think, "This is gonna be good," and I'd start telling it. Suddenly I realized that this Jack tale had all the elements that had excited me in the first fairy tales I heard. I'll let you be the judge of that too.

Now, Jack lived with his mother, his father, and his two brothers, Tom and Will. For at least 20 years the family lived on a farm *waaaaay* up in the mountains. Now, Jack . . . well, he wanted to be like his brothers, hahaaaaah *laaazy,* you know. *(chuckle)* MmMmmm.

His brothers hated work.
Every morning Jack's father would say, *(deep voice)*
"Come on, boys, let's go to work."
And Tom would say, *(whining)* "Oh, but, Daddy, I don't *wanna* go to work."
Will would say, "I'll get up in a minute."
Jack watched this.
Jack's father tired of begging the boys to get up. So he thought, "Oh, my knee baby, he will get up." So he went over to Jack and he said,
"Get up, son. Time to go to work."
Jack would turn over and look at his dad and say, "I don't *wanna* go to work, Daddy."
But Jack's dad would not take that from him. He pulled the covers back and *(clap hands)* gave Jack a big *whack! "GET UP, BOY!"*
And Jack said, *(scared, real quick)* "I'm up, *I'm up.*"
Now, Jack's work was simple. Milk one cow, bring in two buckets of water from the well, then cut up some wood. That's all he had to do. But it took him all day long to do those simple things.
Well, Jack tired of that.
Tom and Will would get away with not working,

". . . and gave Jack a big WHACK!"

LONG JOURNEYS AND QUESTS: *In this very old story, Jack is the youngest child, the knee baby who just got off his mama's lap and has started to walk around. The oldest child is already up and going, but that youngest baby sticks close to his mama's knee.*

In a Jack tale, Jack could come from anywhere or live anywhere, just so Jack is the trickster. He's the one in the story who is lowest on the totem pole, but he always comes out the winner. Any story will work as a Jack tale as long as you have a trickster character who takes a long journey, a real odyssey, but then finally wins the fair maiden or finds the gold.

and saying they didn't want to work, but not Jack.

Jack said, "Enough is enough, I'm running away."

So one morning, *eeeeeeearly* in the morning, Jack put on his bibbed overalls, put on his T-shirt, pulled on his hat, and slipped from the window. Well now, Jack had not been away from home a lot, so after he passed the two-mile marker, he was lost.

"Well," he was thinking, "I should've waited before I ran off. I should've eaten breakfast first."

He was getting a little hungry.

He said to a man that he passed on the road, "Excuse me, sir. *Ahem!* I'm Jack. D'ya know where I can find me some breakfast?"

The man said, "Why don't you go down there to the Army post? Maybe they'll give you breakfast."

Jack said, "That's a good idea."

Soon Jack found himself at the Army post.

The Sergeant said, *(sternly)* "Yep, whatcha want?"

Jack said, *(happy grin)* "I want some breakfast."

"Well," said the Sergeant, "if you eat breakfast around here, you have to be in the Army."

Jack said, "All right, how do I get in the Army?"

The Sergeant said, "Well now . . ."

He turned around, picked up a pencil and a piece of paper. "D'you see that dotted line right there?"

Jack said, "Yeah, I do."

The Sergeant said, "Sign there."

So Jack wrote *(writing motions, very slow)* J—A—C—K.

Jack said, "Now, what does that mean?"

The Sergeant said, "It means you're in the Army."

Jack said, "Does it mean I can get breakfast too?"

The Sergeant said, "Yep, come on in."

"Yep, whatcha want?"

As Jack tales were passed down for many years, they grew very long and involved. Soldier Jack seems to go on forever. These tales almost always start with Jack leaving home to perform some sort of task, and they kind of wander all over the place like Jack does. The tales began in Scotland and England hundreds of years ago and they gathered, with parts coming from all over. So what you hear are all sorts of old English stories, sometimes even little bits of Shakespeare.

The Sergeant said, "But before that, let me explain something to you. We ain't fightin' no wars, so we ain't payin' no money. We will give you some food three times a day, give you a clean uniform, and we'll give you a bed to sleep on."

Jack said, *(big smile)* "That's fine with me."

Well, that started Jack's career in the Army. He slept every night, he had three meals every day, and he always had clean clothes.

Jack stayed in the Army for ten solid years, and enjoyed what the Army was doing for him.

But one day Jack said, "Enough of this, I think I need to get on out and go back home."

Well now, just before Jack left the Army, his parents had passed away. So Jack knew that his brothers Tom and Will were still at home.

". . . I can get breakfast too?"

So he was goin' home. He said to the Sergeant,
    "Sergeant, I've been in the Army long enough.
I think I'd like to get out."

    The Sergeant said, "It's all right with me,
just a minute." He turned around, picked up a piece
of paper, and handed Jack a pencil.

    Jack said, "What do I do with this?"

    The Sergeant said, "Erase your name."

    Jack erased *(erasing motions, very slow)* *J—A—C—K*.

    Jack said, "What does that mean?"

    "It means you're out of the Army."

    Jack said, "Well, thank you, I'll be going now."

    The Sergeant said, "Wait a minute, we have to
help you on your way. Here's a new suit, put it on.
And we're giving you two loaves of bread."

    "Oh," Jack said, "I want this suit, it's a *fine* suit.
But why don't you keep them loaves of bread?"

    "No," the Sergeant said, "this here is what
we give you when we don't pay no money.
This will help you till you find your own bread."

    "Oh," Jack said. "Well, all right." He put them
two loaves of bread under his arm and started home.
(walk your fingers) And he walked and he walked
and he walked and he walked and he walked
and he walked and he walked. *(pause)* And he *walked*
and he walked and he walked and he walked
and he walked and he walked and he walked.

    Well, Jack was getting tired.

    He was knowing that his home was *waaaaaay* up
in the hills and he had a long long walk to go.
But then, *just* as he was headed toward the hills,
he happened to see a man standing beneath a tree.

"... he walked, and he walked ..."

▬▬▬▬▬▬▬▬▬▬

*Oh, children do love this, they love
the time you take with this sort of
thing, the sighs and all. They get a
real sense of journey. Jack always
has a lot of traveling to do, he gets
tired all the time, and children like
to feel they're taking the trip too.*

This man had a piece of wood in his hand, and a pocketknife. He was standing there working on that piece of wood. Jack came up to him and said, "How do you do?"

The man said, "Howdy, Jack."

He *seeeemed* (squint with suspicion) to know Jack.

Jack said, "Whatcha doin'?"

The man said, "I'm whittlin' on a piece of wood."

Jack said, "Heh, heh. Oh. That's nice."

And the man said, "What are *you* doing?"

"Well, I just got out of the Army," Jack said. "I'm on my way home. But I don't know if I'm going to make it or not. I got two brothers up there and they're pretty lazy. I was thinking, if I go there, that'll be three of us that ain't no good. Maybe I got to find me another home somewhere."

"He SEEEEMED to know Jack."

The old man said, "What's that you got there beneath your arm?" So Jack had to look. *(look)*

"Heh, heh," Jack said, "that's my loaf of bread that they give me in the Army."

The old man said, "Son, I'm kinda hungry. Do you think you can give me some of that bread?"

"Oh," Jack said, "I'll do better than that, I'll give you the whole loaf. It's just going to get sweaty here up under my arm if I keep carryin' it."

So he handed the old man the loaf of bread.

The man said, "You know, it ain't many people that would part with a *whole* loaf of bread like this."

And the man said, "I appreciate that, Jack. Now I'm going to give *you* somethin'."

Jack said, "No, that's all right, mmm, heh, heh. You don't have to give me nothin'."

"Why don't you want to take what I give you?"

"'Cause it would be somethin' else to carry."

The old man said, "Don't you worry about that. I'll show you something," and he opened his coat.

He had on a real *fine* pair of galluses. Now, around one of his gallus buttons he had a string, and on that string hung a sack. He unwound that string from his gallus button, took the sack, and he said,

"Watch *this*."

He opened the sack, beat on the side of it, *(beat twice)* and he said, "*Whickety whack get into my sack.*"

And that loaf of bread just lifted up in the air and dropped down to the bottom of the sack.

"*Wooweeeeee!* That's a magic sack," Jack said.

And the man said, "Ha*haaah!* Yes it is. All you have to do is say the magic words and beat

"Wooweee! That's a magic sack."

That's right, I don't show that magic sack, I don't use props at all really, props get in my way. My props are my hands and my face and my eyes, and in the way I gesture and move my body. I want to leave everything to the children's imagination, I want them to think about these things. Then they will see them. I want them to look at me and then they will see Jack and feel like Jack.

The word "gallus" appears a few times in this story, but the word is too nice to change. So I use it, but sometimes I stop and explain that galluses were suspenders that buttoned to a man's pants.

on the side of the sack. Whatever you want to catch will jump right into it. Haha*haaaaaaaaaaaaaaaaah*."

Jack said, "I think I'm going to keep that."

And Jack took the sack, pulled that string tight, wrapped it *(wrap in circles)* around his own gallus button, said goodbye to the old man, and went on his way.

Soon it was very late in the evening. Jack had walked a long way, and he was tired again. But he came up on another fellow standing beneath a tree, leaning on a walking cane.

And Jack said, *(wave hello)* "How ya doin'?"

The man said, *(wave back hello)* "How d'ya do, Jack?"

He *seeeemed (squint)* to know Jack.

And Jack said, "What are you doing?"

The man said, "I'm leaning on my walking cane."

"Oh," Jack said. "Well, I'm on my way home. But I don't think I'm gonna find my home tonight."

The man said, "Well, before you leave here, tell me what you got there beneath your arm."

Jack said, "It's a loaf of sweaty bread."

The man said, "D'ya think you could pick around in there and find me a dry piece?"

"I'll do better than that," Jack said. "I'm going to give you the whole loaf of bread."

The man said, "You know what? I *pegged* you as a fine fellow," he said. "I appreciate this, it ain't many folks that would give up their bread like that."

"Well," Jack said, "I'm glad I could do it for you, it's just something I won't have to carry."

The man said, "I want to pay you back for it."

"No, that's all right, I don't want nothing."

"*You can see the DEATH Angel …*"

And I don't show the magic glass either, I only show Jack looking at it. No prop, only a gesture that seems to hold something small. I'm adding the elements the story will need to work, I'm building up that story triangle. The story has a long way to go before Jack has to pull that magic glass out, but everybody knows he will need that glass before this story is all done; the only question is when.

The man said, "I want to give you something."

Jack said, "Here we go again. Okay, what is it?"

The man reached way down into his pocket and pulled out a little old flat narrow glass. *(hold up your hand)*

He handed it to Jack. Jack turned it over.

Jack looked up in it, and he looked down in it, and then he said, "It ain't made for drinking, is it?"

"Oh no," the man said. "All you do is pour fresh spring water down into this glass, and look in it. You can see the *Death* Angel anywhere it stands."

"Hoo*hoooo*," Jack said. *(pause)* "Why would I want to see the Death Angel?" And the man said,

"You never know, *(shake finger)* *you never know*."

Jack said, "You give it to me, I'm gonna keep it."

So Jack put the glass in his pocket, said goodbye to the old man, and he went on his way.

"You never know, you never know."

When he rounded a curve in the road, he saw a boardinghouse up ahead. "This is where I'll spend the night," Jack said. He knocked on the door, and a woman opened it. "Yes? *(cross arms) What is it?*"

Jack said, "Ma'am, aah, I just got out of the Army. See my new suit? I'm Jack. I don't have no money," he said, "but could I spend the night here?"

"Well, this here is a boardinghouse," she said. "If you have no money, you have no place to stay.

"Now, *get out of here!*" she said.

"Oh, ma'am, *please*," Jack said. "I'm just so . . ."

But the woman said, "No, I don't take nobody in my boardinghouse who hasn't got any money. *Now, get out of here!*" And she slammed the door.

"Well," Jack said, "I thought I might have to sleep in the woods." He followed a fence that went deep into the woods, and put some leaves around a post. He settled back *(lean back, close eyes)* and closed his eyes.

But just as Jack was trying to sleep, he heard a strange noise. *(open one eye)* He opened one eye, and then *(open the other eye)* he opened the other eye. And there, seated on the fence, just above Jack, were seven great big fat turkeys . . . *wild turkeys.*

Jack said, "Look at *that!*"

He opened his coat, unwound that string from around his gallus button, opened that sack, pointed it in the direction of the turkeys, and said,

"*Whickety whack (beat twice) get into my sack.*" One by one, all seven of them great big fat turkeys leaped into the sack. Jack quickly tied it up, leaped over the fence, and ran back to the boardinghouse.

He knocked on the door, and the woman said,
　　"It's *you* again. *(wide eyes)* *Get on out of here!*"
　　Jack said, "Lady, look in this sack." *(extend your hand)*
　　She grabbed the sack and she looked in it.
　　"*Hahaaaaah!* It's *turkeys* in there," she said.
　　Jack said, "Do you want 'em?"
　　She said, "Do I want them? I *need* them.
I don't *ever* have enough turkeys. If you give me
them turkeys, I'll pay you for 'em."
　　She weighed the turkeys, and paid Jack enough
to spend the night in the boardinghouse, eat supper,
get up in the morning and eat breakfast, and have
some change left over. The next morning Jack said,
　　"This is a real nice town. I'll bet you I could
find me a nice house to live in."
　　The woman said, "Well, if you don't, come back,
ha*haaaaah*. And bring me some more turkeys."
　　Well, Jack went looking.

He searched all day long in the town for
a nice house. He went into the caves,
he went up all the mountains, but he
couldn't find a house. He was coming
back to the boardinghouse again when he saw a man
standing in front of this *huuuuge* house.
　　It was the biggest house Jack had ever seen.
It was so *big* *(eyes and arms wide)* it looked like a castle.
　　Jack thought, "I never seen a house so beautiful."
　　And he walked up to the man and he said, *(excited)*
"Sir, this is a *beautiful* house, ain't it?"
　　And the man said, *(bored and quiet)* "Yep, it is."
　　"Reminds me *(eyes wider, more excited)* of the kinda house

where a King and Queen would live," Jack said.

And the man said, "Yep, you're right."

Jack said, "Who lives in a house as fine as this?"

And the man said, *(still bored)* "Nobody."

Jack said, "Do you mean this house is empty?"

And the man said, "Yep, it is."

"Oo*hooooo*," Jack said. "Then it's for sale?"

The man said, "Nope, it isn't."

Jack said, "Well, if it ain't for sale, can I rent it?"

And the man said, *(shake head)* "Unh uh."

Jack said, "I can't rent the house? I can't buy the house? *(puzzled frown)* Who *owns* this house?"

The man said, *(open eyes wide)* "I do."

Jack said, "You own the house, and I can't rent it, and you're not going to let me *buy* it?"

"The man said, 'I'll give it to you.'" The man said, *(point at listener)* "I'll give it to you."

Jack said, "*Hah. Noooo.* You wouldn't *give* me this big old pretty house. What do I do to get it?"

The man said, *(lift a finger)* "Just spend one night in it."

Jack said, "One night? Spend one night in it? That's all? Mmmm. What's wrong with the house?"

The man said, "It's *(pause, look both sides)* *hainted.*"

Jack said, *(panicky)* "*Hainted?* Hainted with what?"

The man said, *(pause, look both sides again)* "Haints."

Jack said, *(whisper)* "Haints? What *kind* of Haints?"

"Little ol' bitty green ones." *(fingers show tiny size)*

Jack said, "I never seen a green Haint before."

The man said, "Well, they's in there. If you go in, they'll eat you up, and you'll be a green Haint too."

Jack said, "Well, let me tell you, I ain't never been scared of Haints, green or otherwise," he said. "I'm goin' in there and I'm gonna spend the night. Haaah. This house is going to be *mine* tomorrow."

The man said, "Let me give you a little advice. Do you *(pointing)* have anything to eat?"

Jack said, "Well, I was gonna ask if you could provide a picnic lunch for me, and aaaaah, maybe a corncob pipe with some tobacco to smoke?"

The man said, "Let me give you more advice. You better eat that picnic lunch before nine o'clock, and smoke that pipe before ten o'clock, and get all your sleeping done before twelve o'clock, 'cause after that, them Haints are gonna eat you up."

Jack said, "Let me be the judge of that, thank ya."

So the man brought him the picnic lunch and the corncob pipe and a quilt to sleep on too. Then the man left the house and locked the door.

And Jack could hear him going down the road,

"Haints? What KIND of Haints?"

▬▬▬▬▬▬▬▬▬▬

Hah! The little green Haints were my favorite growing up. I heard the term first from Grandpa, then my teachers told stories about green Haints. I thought they were wonderful. "Oh yes, tell us more about the Haints," we'd say, and of course, the teacher would read more into those little things than was written in the stories 'cause she knew we liked them so much. And so can you. Children will ask lots of questions, you know, and you can add on whatever comes to mind, just like my teachers did.

"Aaaahaaaaa*aaaaaaaaaaaahahahahahaha.*"

And Jack said, *(big eyes, sort of scared)* "*Uh oh.*"

But Jack didn't let on that he was scared.
He reached into the picnic basket and got the pipe,
began to pack tobacco in it, *(stuff finger into fist)* then he
scratched a match, and was trying to light that pipe.
But ya know, if you've ever smoked a corncob pipe,
them brand-new ones, they don't puff easily.

So Jack emptied that pipe with a knife, *(blow into hand)*
trying to find out what was keepin' it from puffin'.
As he was cleaning it out, he heard something.
Waaaaaaaaaaaaay down in the cellar.

And it sounded like,
*Whoo**whoooooooo**haaa**hahahaaa**aaaaaaaaaa.*

And Jack said, "Uh oh." But he didn't let on like
he was scared, he just kept cleanin' that pipe.

"And Jack said, 'UH OH.'"

Then after a while, he heard something again. *Waaaaaaaay* up in the attic.

*Whoo**hoopwhoo**hoopoo**hahahaa**aaaaaaaa.*

And Jack said, "Oh no." But he kept on cleaning that pipe. Then after a while he heard a great big roaring sound, something roaring down the chimney.

Whooooooooosh!

And suddenly, right there before Jack, rolled a *great* big old green ball. And out of the middle of that green ball popped *seven* . . . green . . . Haints.

Jack could say nothing but, "How do you do?"

"***What're ya*** *doin' in this house?*" they said.

Jack said, *(quiet and timid)* "*Ummm,* I'm gonna spend the night in this house, and when I've spent the night, this house *(point at yourself)* is going to be mine."

And the Haints said, "No it ain't. **Hahaa***aaaa.* 'Cause we're gonna eat you up *(lots of glee) tonight.*"

Jack said, "I ain't scared of you, I ain't scared. You ain't gonna run me off. *(stubborn and determined)* I ain't scared of Haints. I just *ain't* scared of 'em."

Well, the Haints saw that Jack was not afraid, so they knew they'd have to do something to get their house back. So they all got in a huddle and they started talking. *(turn head side to side)*

*Mumbly**mumbly**mumum**umbly**mumbly.*

*Mum**blymum**blymu**mumumbly**mumbly.*

The head Haint kept looking back at Jack. They decided what to do. The head Haint said,

"All right, seeing as how you ain't scared of us, we're gonna play a game of cards with ya."

Jack said, "Well, *(pause)* all right."

"If we win, we gonna eat you up," the Haint said.

**"WHOOOOOOOOOOSH!
And suddenly, right there . . ."**

Oh yes, those Haints really had to be green. If you walk around in the woods or the swamp, you can see green slime on pine trees and the nasty green moss that grows there. The Haints were damp and cold and nasty, so it was natural they'd all be green slimy fellows.

"I been in the Army for *10 years*," Jack said. "I learned to play cards real good. What if I win?"

"We still gonna eat you up." (big menacing eyes)

Jack said, "That sounds fair."

So they all sat down, and the Haints commenced to puttin' great big stacks of yellow gold nuggets in front of them on the table.

"Now, wait," Jack said. "I can't play cards, I don't have anything in my pocket but a few pennies."

They said, "We'll give you some gold."

And all seven Haints stood up, held their fingers out, and they made (many stacking motions) stacks and piles and stacks and piles of gold all over the floor. They gave Jack half, and they kept the other half.

And this was how the game went:

Jack would win a hand, (point to the right) and the Haints would win a hand. (point to the left)

Jack would win a hand, (point to the right) and the Haints would win a hand. (point to the left)

Jack would win a hand, (point both hands to the right) and the Haints would win a hand. (both hands to the left)

Jack would win a hand, (both hands to the right) and the Haints would win a hand. (both hands to the left)

Well, Jack just got plum tired of that. He stood up, opened his coat, unwound that string from around his gallus button, opened the sack, pointed it in the direction of the Haints, and he said,

"*Whickety whack!* (beat twice) *Get into my sack!*"

And one by one, all seven of them green Haints leaped down into the bottom of that old sack.

Jack tied it up and threw it behind the door. He smoked his corncob pipe, laid down on his quilt,

*"'We still gonna eat you up.'
Jack said, 'That sounds fair.'"*

Jack tales can be scary, if you really think about them, but they can be funny too. You can add all sorts of odd things and you can stretch them out too. Like the card game. You want children to really see Jack playing with those strange little Haints, so stretch it out. They will laugh at the game, just like they'll laugh when Jack says, "That sounds fair," when the Haints tell him they will eat him up no matter what happens.

and slept for the rest of the night.

The next morning Jack heard the door opening.

Click click, creeeeeeeeeeeeeeaaak.

And the man walked in. He was scared 'cause he knew the Haints had eaten Jack all up. But Jack jumped up. *(big yawn and stretch)*

"*Hoowwhooooaaaaaaaaaaa.*"

"**YEOOOOW!**" the man said. "*You're still alive.*"

Jack said, "Well, did you think I wouldn't be?"

The man said, "But them Haints . . . them *Haints.* Didn't they eat you up?"

"Nooo," Jack said. "Here, take this to the river." He handed the man the sack. *(hold hand out)*

"Find the deepest end," Jack said, "open the sack, and drop 'em in. And bring my sack back."

The man said, *(timid)* "What's in here?"

"'YEOOOOW!' the man said."

Jack said, "Them Haints."

The man said, "*Oooo*, don't give 'em to *meeeeee*."

"Go on now," said Jack.

And so the man went down to the river, found the deepest end, and dropped the Haints in. He brought the sack back and gave it to Jack.

He said, "The house is yours. You deserve it."

So Jack went into the house, and low and behold, them Haints had left *every* piece of that gold.

Jack had him a brand-new house, a *castle*, and he was a rich man to boot. He had so much gold,

he buried some up under the house,

he hoarded some between the walls,

he put some under his mattress,

and he put the rest in his pocket.

Jack was a wealthy man. Ha*haaaaaaaaaa*.

"They'd just wave back and . . ."

Again, as you tell a story about Jack's long journeys, think about the things that all children like. Remember the universal truths, the emotions of love, hate, and fear we all know. If a King in the story was a wicked King, oh, the children all want to hate villains. If Jack was in love, all children like to hear stories about love.

B ut you know, Jack was a very *lonely* man. The *only* woman that he liked was the King's daughter. And she liked Jack too. But she wouldn't let on that she did.

She'd sit on the King's porch and *(wave)* she'd wave.

They'd just wave back and forth all the time.

One day Jack was figurin' he had enough money, he had a nice home, he'd ask the King's daughter to marry him. But when he got to the King's house, the King's daughter wasn't on the front porch.

"She's probably inside," Jack said.

He knocked *(knock)* and the King opened the door.

"Well, well. It's *Jack*," the King said.

And Jack said, "Howdy, King."

"Well, Jack, I'm not doin' so well. *(sob, sob)* *Hohoo*."

Jack said, "King, why are you crying like that?"

"I'm not doing so well. HOHOO."

Believe it or not, even little boys like love stories if you pick the right one. But there has to be a lot of adventure in it. That's why the Prince in fairy tales had to accomplish at least four quests before he could marry the fair maiden. He had to capture the golden fleece, he had to ride the magic grasshopper, he had to fight giants and dragons to get that one magic thing before he could marry the Princess. As long as the story has adventures in it, the love story will work.

And the King said, "It's m'child, *(sob)* *it's m'child.*
She's real, real sick. The doctor says she'll die."

"Oh," Jack said. "I'm sorry."

The King said, "Jack, what are you doing here?"

Jack said, "Well, sir. Umm. I've come to ask you
for your daughter's hand in marriage."

The King said, "Waahoohoo*hooohoooooo.*
She's going to be *dead* before she can get married."

"Oh," Jack said, "I'm so sorry. Do you think
I could see her before she dies?"

"You better hurry," said the King. "The doctor
says the Death Angel is in the room with her."

Jack said, "All right, I'll . . . I'll go see her."

So Jack ran down the hall to the daughter's room.
He opened the door and there she was in the bed,
all stretched out, low, low sick. Jack went to the bed.

". . . he poured the water into . . ."

Beside the bed was a table and pitcher and bowl. Jack looked into the pitcher and inside that pitcher was fresh spring water. So he went into his pocket and got his glass, and he *(pour into hand)* poured the water into the glass, and held that glass up.

He looked *all* around the room, and he saw it. Standing there behind the daughter's bed, ready to grab her at any moment, was *the Death Angel.*

Awwwwwwwwwk! Jack stepped back.

He unbuttoned his coat, unwound that string from around his gallus button, took that sack and pointed it at the Death Angel.

"Whickety whack! (beat twice) Get into my sack!"

The Death Angel flew up into the air, and down into the sack. Jack tied that sack closed, then ran out the door, down the road, and deep into the woods.

". . . and held that glass up."

___

The Death Angel. This is another religious reference from the Bible that appears in Jack tales, and again it's from Revelations. "And I saw a bright angel fall from heaven and in one hand he held the key, and in the other the chains that would tie the dragon."

He hung the sack in the *tallest* oak tree he could find.

When Jack got back, the King's daughter was up, alive and well. So Jack and the King's daughter got married, and they lived and lived and they lived. Jack lived to be 600 years old. Yes, he did.

One morning Jack walked along the road, and he spotted an old man. This man was so old, he was bent half in two and his nose was dragging along the ground.

"Howdy, old daddy. What's the matter witcha?"

The man said, *(angry)* "I'm *old*, can't you see that?"

"Yessir, I can see that. How old are you?"

The man said, "At last count, I'm 600 years old."

"Oooh," Jack said. "Why didn't you die before you got to be 600 years old?"

"Ain't you heard? Ain't nobody told you? Years ago, some dumbbell tied up the Death Angel in a sack, and since then, *nobody's* been able to die."

Jack said, "Uh oh. Do you reckon that was *me?*"

He got to thinkin' about this. He knew he was too old to climb a tree, so he took his shotgun to the woods, and searched till he found the sack.

Then he *aaaaimed* that shotgun *(squint)* at the sack. He shot three times.

BOOOOOM! BOOOOOM! ***BOOOOOM!***

And one of those shots hit the sack, it started to fall, the top opened, and the Death Angel flew out. *(pause)*

I guess you know that Jack was the first to go.

But he had lived a *looong* and happy life.

... And *that's* the end of that.

"BOOOM! BOOOM! BOOOM!"

I told the story for many years thinking how wonderful it would be to defeat death, how great it would be to hang death in a sack, putting it off as long as I chose. But then I saw in real life what pain and suffering could be like. I thought no, death is necessary when you've used your body up. You had a hundred years in it maybe, so enough, leave it alone, put it to rest. Now I think Jack tricked himself by living too long. Some things that might seem to be good, well, maybe they aren't.

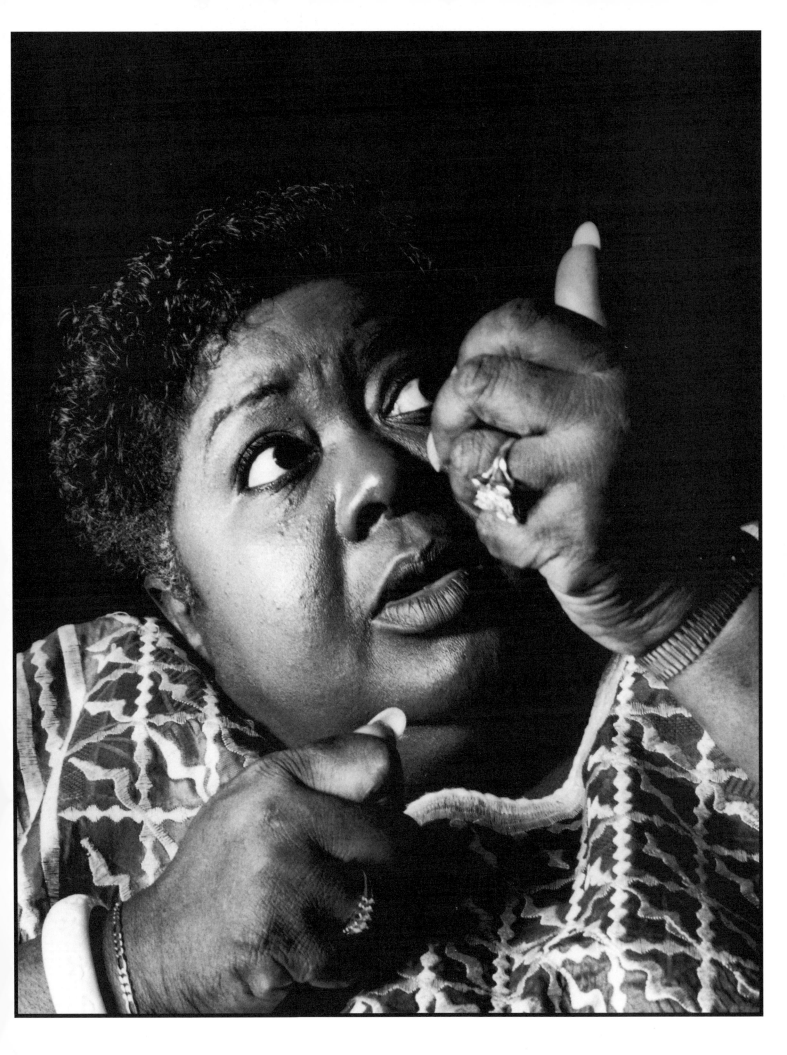

The King

O nce upon a time there was a King;
his name was King.
He had a wife named Queen.
And they had a daughter, Princess.
Everybody in the court, the ladies-in-waiting and all,
they would take time out while they were in court
for little Princess. They'd catch her ball, you know,
and they'd fuss over Princess and kiss her,
and then Princess would go on about her way,
and the daily rigors of court would go on.

The Queen

The Princess

"Once upon a time there was . . ."

VISUALIZING YOUR STORIES:
*You really must see the scenes
and your characters in your mind
as you tell a story. Visualize the
story as if you are living in it, not
just talking about it. Believe in
your story, and make things real.
Characters are hard to believe if
they are too perfect, kingdoms
are unreal if they are paradises.*

Every Wednesday, King, who was a good King,
a healthy, wonderful King, and his wife, Queen,
a beautiful woman and very smart, would hold court.
King gave his people time to come in
and brag about what they had grown that week.
Or he gave them time to talk if they were unhappy
about anything, or if somebody mistreated them.
One day, as he was holding court, this farmer
stood up and introduced himself.

And King, who was just so proud of himself because
he knew everybody who lived in his kingdom,
he said to the man, "I know you well."

The man said, "I live *(point)* right down the road."

And King said, "Yes, I know."

"I've got a nice wife, a beautiful woman,"
the man said, "and seven children, cutest little bugs."

"Yes," said the King, "I've seen them all."

"Well, the other day I was plowing," the man said.
"And the Witch that lives up in the hollow, she come
up quick behind me like a thunderstorm. The sky
got dark, it commenced to thunderin' and lightnin'
and carryin' on, I turned around and there she was."

"Well, she's bound to make entrances like that."

"Well, she made one on me," the man said.
"And I want you to know, King, she near scared me
to death. Wanted to buy five of my finest cows.

"Well, I *had* to refuse her," the man said.
"The money sounded good, but I *had* to refuse her.
You see, that's what I feed my children with. And
if I don't have the milk to feed them, they cry. And
if my wife doesn't have milk to make bread, she cries.

"Well, that made the Witch real mad.

"She put a curse on my cows and dried 'em up."
The man said, "They's giving nothin' but blood now."

"Oh," the King said, *(angry)* "that's horrible."

"Well," the man said, *(spread hands)* "I couldn't do
nothing but come to you for your help. I want you
to know that my children are crying day and night,
and my wife won't stop at all."

"So that's where all that noise was coming from,"
the King said. "I'm sorry.

"King, who was just so proud . . ."

See everything clearly as you
describe it, and kids will believe
it's happening. Now, King in this
story has a problem, but you can
tell he's right on top of it. He acts
like a real person, and he cares
about his people. You can show
that with expressions and voices.
King wants people to come and
talk about their problems, but he
also wants to hear what a good
job he's doing. That's his ego.
King wants to show how brilliant
he is, and that makes him real.

". . . that made the Witch real mad."

When I tell stories about witches,
I think of them as cold, very cold,
and I hear screeching sounds.
Witches are evil from head to toe,
they are hateful and sinister-like.
If you want to project a strong
image like that, you gotta feel it,
you gotta have a very definite
feeling about witches. And you
really have to show it. Oh my yes,
children do love to hate mean
witches, so you help them along.

I'm gonna have something done about her."

The King turned to his soldiers.

"Go up to the hollow," he said. *(furious)* "Tie her to a horse, tie her to two horses, put her on a wagon, I don't care how, but *YOU GET HER HERE!* I'm tired of hearing about this wicked Witch."

Well, the soldiers saluted the King and went off.

The King said, "Now, until we get her back here, you have a seat and I'll call on somebody else."

And sure enough, people started talking again, one after the other, standing up, when all at once the King heard something out on his front porch.

Baaaaaaaaaaa YAAAAAAAEEeeeeeerk!

King said, "Excuse me a moment, *what was that?*"

The King listened. *(pause)* It was quiet.

He said to the people, "Well, go right ahead."

"BaaaaaaYAAAAAAEEeeeeerk!"

Yes, you have to think just like a witch, disliking everybody and hating everybody. You'd never want anybody to say yes to you, you're glad when people say no because then you get revenge. You enjoy hurting people, you like to see them bleed, especially young men. Old men have hurt themselves in some way already, it's young men you want to get.

The Wicked Witch

They started up, but the same sound came again. *Baaaaa**aaaaa**YAAAAAAAEEee**eeeerk!*

King said, "Excuse me." *(pause)* He listened again. Suddenly, the double doors of the main courtroom flew open, and a terrible *(arms twirling)* cold whirlwind *bolted* into the middle of the room.

"*Hey* there, what is this?" the King said.

The wind stopped. There was the wicked Witch. *Baaaaa**aaaaa**YAAAAAAAEEee**eeeerk!*

"Oh, *Lord have mercy*, woman!" said the King. "Do you really *(raise arms high)* *have* to do that?"

She said, *(point finger)* "*DID YOU SEND FOR ME?*"

King said, "Yes, I did."

She said, "Well, *(shake finger furiously)* you better tell me what you want before I get ready to go."

"You're not going anywhere," the King said.

"Oh, yes I am," the Witch said. "You got no right to summon me down here. I have things to do."

He said, "The only thing *you* got to do is sit down and wait till I'm finished with this gentleman."

The Witch started to scream and holler and yell and curse and carry on something awful.

It was really bad.

King said, "We have to deal with her right now." He said to the Witch, "Do you know this man?"

The Witch said, "I ain't never seen him before."

"You tellin' me you don't *recognize* this man?"

"I'm tellin' you I never seen him in my life."

The King said, "Are you telling me you did not cause his cows to drain blood?"

The Witch said, *(eyes very wide)* "*NO!*"

The King said, "Are you telling me the truth?"

"DID YOU SEND FOR ME?"

Yes, to do a real good bad witch you have to visualize a bad witch. You have to feel like you had no mother and father, or if you did, they were very cruel and left you out in the woods. And you have no children either, or you'd eat them. To a bad witch, children are chubby and fat, and they are delicious with sugar or molasses.

And the Witch said, *(cackle)* "*Baaahaaah!* No."

"Enough," the King said. "Whether you're telling me the truth or not, I have heard enough from you. I am going to sentence you to hang by your thumbs until you take off some of these evil spells . . ."

The Witch said, "If I were you, I'd be careful."

Just at that time the doors of the court opened, and in walked little Princess, bouncing her ball.

It was too late.

Everybody looked at Princess at the same time.

The Queen said, *(afraid)* "Princess, *go back*, my dear."

The King said, *(loud and quick)* "*Go out*, my dear."

And the Witch said, "*Whoohahayahooooo*."

She pointed *(point)* at the little girl. Princess stopped.

She looked cold as ice and hard as a rock.

"... in walked little Princess..." The King ran from the throne and touched his child.

He said, *(whimpering)* "She's turned to *stone*."

And the Queen began to cry.

Everybody in the court got up to touch Princess.

The wicked Witch stood there.

"Are you *through* with me?" she said.

The King said, "What have you done to my child? This child *(afraid and angry)* has done you no wrong."

"Let me go," she said. "I have things to do."

The King said, "Quick, send me my physicians."

The guards went out and brought 25 physicians. The King began to talk to them in whispering tones. *Whisphisspywhissssp. Whisphisspywhissssp.*

The physicians gathered around little Princess, and they scratched her and touched her, and they *(sniff and sniff)* smelled her, and they *(lap and lap)* licked her, and then they stood before the King. *(straighten back)*

"We have come to one conclusion," they said. "She's been turned to stone." *(nod positively)*

The King said, "Get out of here! I *know* that. Send me *(commanding)* the wise men of the kingdom."

So 40 wise men came to court and whispered with the King. *Whisssssssphisspy, whisssspyhissssp.*

The wise men gathered about little Princess, and they stroked her head, and they touched her, and they *(sniff, sniff)* smelled her and *(lap, lap)* tasted her, and then they read a long proclamation.

"She's been turned to stone!" *(nod twice positively)*

The King said, "I *knew* that. *Get out of here!*"

He said to the Witch, "What do you want of me?"

"Well," said the Witch. "*Whooohaaaaaaaaa!* I haven't had such a good time in about 200 years. I'll tell you what, *haaaaaa*, let's have a little contest.

"What have you done to my child?"

Poor King. He has 25 physicians and 40 wise men scratching his daughter and sniffing her, but all they tell him is what he already knows. Now the kingdom has a bigger problem. This is how a good Jack tale works; a problem turns into a quest, an adventure. By this time, if you are seeing and telling your story clearly, your listeners will be deeply involved. Don't be afraid to enter the story, to really become the characters.

You send some young men up to my house with 1,000 dollars in gold to put up for a contest. *Haaaaa!* If they *win*, (snicker) I'll take every one of them spells I cast in the last 100 years off your folks.

"Otherwise, (glare) they'll be *dead. Hahaaa!*"

Well, the King sent a proclamation to every nook and cranny in the kingdom; 1,000 dollars would get a young man into the contest.

And the King added a little. If a man should win, he would give the hand of Princess in marriage, and he would give a third of his kingdom.

This proclamation went *all* the way up the hills to where Jack and his brothers lived.

Well, Jack's brothers thought if the old Witch was 200 years old, surely as young men they would win.

Well, their father was quite interested, so he took the family savings, which was just about 1,000 dollars in gold, and he gave it to Will and Tom.

And they set out.

It was a long ways to the wicked Witch's house, and about midways they stopped to rest. You see, Jack's mama had packed a lunch. There was ham and corn bread and sweet water.

As they ate, an old man walked up to them and he said, (crackly voice) "Good day to you, my boys."

And Tom and Will said, "Howdy, old fella."

"You know," the man said, "I'm a little hungry. Could you give me some of your food?"

"Ummm, we don't have enough."

"Well, I'm a little thirsty, could I have some . . ."

"We drank the last drop."

"Otherwise, they'll be DEAD."

As long as I tell this story, I am going to make you see this witch as mean, hateful, and deceitful. That's important. But you know, once I ran into a group of witches who were picketing me, they thought I was unfair to witches. They said they weren't like that. Well, I'm sure that they weren't, but I don't choose to change, that's the story. Now I'm waiting for the giants to come after me.

"*Oooo*," said the old man, "you are a stingy lot."
He said, *(sinister)* "And life will be most stingy to you."
And the old man disappeared.
Tom said to Will, "Did you see *that?*"
Will said to Tom, *(nodding)* "Uh huh."

They went on and made it to the Witch's house.
There they saw a long line of young men, a line going
all the way around and through the Witch's house.
Tom and Will took their place in the line.
All the men stood there with 1,000 dollars in gold.
The line moved slowly. Maybe every 30 minutes
they could hear something that sounded like
AaaaaaahOoooaaaaahOooooooo!
And Tom said to Will, "Did you hear *that?*"
And Will said to Tom, *(horrified)* "Uh huh."

"And the old man disappeared."

You see, Tom and Will had been selfish. They didn't help the old man who was going to help them, they wouldn't give him anything. So he couldn't give them what they needed to journey on with. As the saying goes, if you have your hand closed, then nothing goes out and nothing comes in.

I don't think you really need a hackleblade to tell this story, not if you describe it well enough. As I said earlier, I really don't like props too much, I want people to think about these things when I talk about them. But sometimes I will show the hackleblade; it's a part of country living and I love how sharp and horrible it looks. But always remember, if a prop is too gimmicky, it will distract the children and they won't listen to your story. For example, if you play an instrument, then do use it, but beware. Too much music and kids may think, "Oh no, she's not gonna sing again, is she?"

Finally Tom and Will were in the front of the line. The Witch walked over. "Good *day*, sweet boys. *Wooo*. Didya come to do contest with ol' Mama?"

And Tom said to Will, *(whisper)* "You gonna answer?"

And Will said to Tom, "*You* answer."

"Ye-ye-yes, ma'am, *(stutter)* we di-did."

She said, "*Hah!* Did you bring your money?"

"Ye-ye-yes, ma'am, *(stutter)* we di-did."

"Well then, *(point up high) throw it on the pile.*"

The pile was at least as tall as a boulder. So Tom took the 1,000 dollars in gold and threw it on top.

"Woo*wooooo*," the wicked Witch said. "Now come, boys, I'll show you how easy it is to win."

They followed the Witch to the end of the fence. There she picked up a terrible-looking thing, and she said, "Do you see this sweet thing? *Hmm?*"

And Tom said, *(scared stiff)* "Uh-uh-huh."

"*Heeee*," she said. "This *(sinister glint)* is a *hackleblade*. A sweet thing indeed, isn't it? Well, this is what we do at the contest. I place it on the ground, and you jump up into the air and you land headfirst on the hackleblade. *(sinister howl)* *HOOAAahahaaa.* If you stand without pain, you have won the contest."

Tom said, "But, we'll kill ourselves."

"Oh no, you won't," she said. "Let me show you."

And with that she ran back across the yard. She turned and ran as fast as she could toward the hackleblade, leaped into the air, and threw herself headfirst onto the nails.

For one second she lay there, then she stood up and shook the pain from her head. And she said,

"*Haaaaaa?* See how *easy* that was, my boys?"

Will said to Tom, "Seein' you're the youngest," he said, "why don't you go first?"

Tom said, "Well, you're the oldest. *You* go first."

"No no, *(begging)* you go first," said Tom.

"No no, *(whimpering)* you go first," said Will.

And the Witch said, "One of you better go first, or I will fix it so neither one of you will be here!"

Tom said, "I'll b-be the first."

Tom walked across the yard. It took a long time to get up the steam he needed, but he ran just as quickly as he could toward the hackleblade, then he leaped high, *(raise arms way up)* high up into the air . . .

But he missed with his head. He missed with his shoulder, *(hold shoulder)* and his side hit the nails.

"*AaaaaaHOOOoooowoooooooooh!*"

And the Witch said, "Oh, my my my. He missed.

"This is a HACKLEBLADE."

A hackleblade was used to clear the seeds out of cotton, which made the flax easier to spin. You pulled the cotton through the nails, and then picked the seeds out with a knife or stick. Fancy ones had a handle so you could comb the naps out of a cow's tail. I found this one at a flea market in the mountains of Tennessee, and it has old, hand-made nails.

Haaaaaaa! (long sinister chuckle) *Get him outta here!"*

They pulled the hackleblade from Tom's side. Will was next.

He ran just as fast as he could and up into the air. But he missed with his head, and his shoulder hit the nails. *"AaaaaaHOOOoooooooohhh!"*

"Get him outta here!" said the Witch. *"Next!"*

om and Will returned home, almost dead. Jack was so mad he didn't know what to do. "I *can't* let that wicked Witch do that to my brothers. She just about killed them." Jack's dad said, "Now, settle down, son. Do you see that Tom and Will are almost dead?"

"But I must avenge them," Jack said.

"Daddy, give me 1,000 dollars," he said.

"Son, I have given all I have to your brothers," Jack's dad said. "They lost it. We don't even have enough money to get help for them. They may die."

Jack said, "Well, all right, Daddy. Mama, fix me some sweet water and corn bread and sugar cakes and let me go fight that wicked Witch."

"Son," she said, "there's nothing left (spread arms) but day-old corn bread here, and a little well water."

"That's fine," Jack said, "I'll take it."

So she placed the bread in a sack, and she put the water in a jug, and off Jack went.

His father thought he would never see Jack again.

Jack went a long way. He had no way of knowing that the Witch's house was such a far piece.

So he rested.

As he sat there, an old man came before him.

"... fix me some sweet water ..."

Sweet water has either honey or sugar in it, and kids in the country drank it for energy like kids today might drink Kool-Aid or iced tea. It was carried on your arm in a jug with a corncob plug. When you were ready for it, you'd swing the jug around, pull the plug out, take your drink, and keep walking.

"How do you do, son?" said the old man.

"Oh, I am well," Jack said, "but I am very tired. Why don't you sit down with me?"

"Thank you, my boy," said the old man. "Tell me, what do you have there *(point)* in your sack?"

Jack said, "It's day-old corn bread, but my mama makes good bread. Why don't I share it with you?"

"Oh, thank you," said the old man.

So Jack reached *(reach down)* into the sack. He pulled out what he thought was his corn bread, but it wasn't bread at all, it was sweet molasses cake with honey and butter running out of it.

And Jack said, "Hmm. Why don't you take that? I'll see what else I have in here." *(look down)*

And he pulled another cake from the sack.

So Jack and the man rested and ate sweet cakes

". . . but it wasn't bread at all . . ."

No, it was sweet molasses cake. Mm. Now, how did that happen? Molasses cake was made with sorghum and it was very sweet. It was really cake and it was soft and smelled real good. The King would have molasses cake, with icing made of honey and butter.

with honey and butter. Oh, they were *sooooo* good.

The old man said, "Son, we've got to stop this, my throat's gettin' tight. Whatcha got in your jug?"

Jack said, "Well, I ain't sure. Let's find out."

And Jack lifted the jug and pulled out the cork, threw it over his shoulder and drank. *"Aaaah."* But it wasn't water at all, it was sweet . . . cool . . . wine.

And they passed the wine between them.

"Ooooh," said Jack, "that was wonderful, but I think we should stop now."

The man said, "Yes, I think so too. Now tell me, where are you off to, young man?"

Jack said, "I'm going to fight the wicked Witch."

"Oh," said the old man. "You're joking with me. Do you know how *mean* she is?"

Jack said, "She almost killed my brothers. I'm going to avenge them, they're almost dead."

"Now, young man, you must be very careful," the old man said. "Where is your money?"

Jack said, "I don't have any money, sir. I thought maybe I could get into the contest anyway."

"Let me lend you the money." The old man placed his hand behind him, and from nowhere at all came a sack of 1,000 dollars in gold.

Jack said, "Sir, I'm from a poor family, and I have no way of knowing how to pay you back."

"Do not worry, my boy," said the old man. "You are kind and generous, and that will go far.

"But be careful. Let me give you some advice. Anyone you see on the way to the Witch's house, take them with you. I'll give you a way to travel."

And the old man *(reach in pocket)* went into his pocket,

"Do not worry, my boy . . ."

So the old man pops up again and gives Jack the chance to be kind and generous, just like he did for Jack's brothers. This man is God in the Jack tales, oh yes, most definitely. You see, God gives you a brain, and he gives you the ability to learn so you can get on in the world, so you can live more easily. You always run into people who can provide for you, along the street and in your travels, always. Sometimes they need your help. But if you don't help them, if you don't provide, they likely won't provide for you.

and took out a little carved ship. It was carved
out of wood, and he *(reach down)* placed it on the ground.

Jack said, "What is that?"

The old man said, "That, my dear, is a flying ship.
All you have to say is *(wave hands)* *FLY SHIP, FLY*."

With that, the ship suddenly grew enoo*ooormous*,
and the sails *(wave arms)* began to billow in the wind.

Quickly Jack leaped inside and the ship started
to lift itself up into the air. Jack waved goodbye
to the old man and he said, *(from afar)* "*Thank youuuuu*."

"Remember," said the old man, *(look up and wave)*
"pick up anyone you see on your way."

And so, as Jack rolled along inside the ship,
he looked from side to side trying to see somebody,
but there was no one. He was above the mountains,
then above the trees, then above more mountains.

"... the sails began to billow ..."

Hardy Hardhead

Suddenly there was something going on below him.

There was a man. This man was *leaping* up into the air and hurling himself headfirst into a rock. Then he stood up and *(shake head, cross eyes)* shook it off.

Well, Jack watched that for almost an hour. Then he brought the ship to rest beside the man.

Jack said, *(with wonder)* "What are you doin'?"

The man said, *(silly smile)* "I'm playin'."

Jack said, "What are you playin'?"

And the man said, "Hurl yourself into the rock."

Jack said, "Doesn't that hurt?"

The man said, "*Aaaahmmm.* I don't know."

Jack said, "What's your name?"

Jack

"My name is Hardy Hardhead."
"I thought maybe it might be."

Oh yes, and we always run into somebody like Hardy Hardhead too. He's an ally, somebody who takes us along in life and helps. Sometimes they're not so bright, but they are there and ready to help. Hardy is a good person, his joy in life is hitting rocks with his head; I like Hardy Hardhead a lot.

The man said, "My name is Hardy Hardhead."

Jack said, "I thought maybe it might be."

"Hardy," he said, "would you like to ride with me?"

Hardy said, "Yeah, I would."

Jack said, "Well then, get in."

So Hardy Hardhead leaped into the air, jumped into the ship headfirst, shook his head, and sat up.

"Let's go," he said, *(silly grin)* and off they went.

It took a long time to get to the Witch's house,

but when they arrived Jack brought the ship down. Then he made it small enough to go into his pocket. He took Hardy Hardhead and his 1,000 gold dollars, and they took their place in line.

All you could hear was

AaaaaaahOoooaaaaahOooooooohhhhh!

Hardy Hardhead said to Jack, *(nod and smile)* "Sounds like somebody's having a real good time."

Jack said, "Well, I don't know about that."

Soon they were at the front of the line.

There *(cackle, cackle)* stood the wicked Witch.

"*Heeehaaaahaaaa.* Well, *hello* there, my *pretties.* Did you come to do contest with the Witch? *Haaa.* Come this way. Put your money on the pile."

By now the pile of gold was tall as a mountain, so Jack started another pile of gold beside it.

"This is what you do," the wicked Witch said. And she showed them the hackleblade.

Jack said, "Well, ma'am, do you think my friend Hardy Hardhead could go before me?"

She said, "I don't *CARE* who goes, *just DO IT!*" And she placed the hackleblade on the ground.

Hardy scratched his head. Then he walked *waaaaay* across the yard, ran back as fast as he could, *leaped* into the air, turned three big somersaults, and came down headfirst on the hackleblade. *Stooove* those nails right through the hackleblade, got up, shook his head, and laughed. "*Hoooo*, that was *fun*."

Well, the Witch was so angry, she began to whirl and twirl *(wave arms around)* like a tornado, and before you knew it, she stoved *herself* right into the ground.

Some folks say they have seen her in China.

"... she began to whirl and ..."

And the Witch disappears. Sort of quietly, not gruesomely at all. This is really a fairy-tale ending, a "happily ever after" ending, but you know, kids don't seem to like them so much anymore, they seem to want to deal with reality now. The old fairy tales are just too far-fetched. I can't tell you why, but children want to fight their way out of everything now, not trick or love their way out.

Well, sir, as she went right through the ground, *every* spell she had cast for 100 years was removed, and Princess skipped once again around the court.

Jack and Hardy Hardhead were left standing there with a mountain of gold and the ship.

So they loaded the gold and flew to see the King.

As they landed, the King embraced them both.

"Jack, will you accept my daughter in marriage?"

"Well, sir King, I'm just a boy. I don't think I want to get married yet. But my friend might."

And Hardy Hardhead said, "Well, *(big silly goofy grin)* can she play hurl your head into the rock?"

The King said, *(frown)* "I don't think so."

Hardy said, "Hmm. I don't want her then."

The King said, "Well then, what can I do for you? Do you want to rule my kingdom?"

Jack said, "No, I don't wanna rule your kingdom. But Hardy Hardhead might."

Hardy said, "Has it got any rocks on it? Hmm?"

King said, "No."

Hardy said, "I don't want it then."

The King said, "But what can I *do* for you?"

Jack said, "Well, I got two mighty sick brothers. I could use that money to help them get well."

King said, "You can have every bit of that gold. And if you need any more, you're welcome to it."

And they say that Jack and Hardy Hardhead went home with the gold, took care of Tom and Will, and to this day are living quite well off the money they won from the wicked Witch of the hollow.

. . . And *that's* the end of *that*.

"Has it got any rocks on it?"

That's right, Jack didn't marry Princess and he didn't want the kingdom, and Hardy Hardhead didn't either. But you know, I tell a lot of stories like that, where Jack doesn't win the fair maiden. Because that's the way life is, you deal with what comes along. In this story, Jack wins, but he is only 15 years old. He didn't want to get married, he didn't know anything about ruling a kingdom, so he said, "Well, thank you, King, but I would just like to go home and take care of my brothers." And he did. He took care of his brothers, they were never rich, but that's the way life really is.

W hen Jack was a grown man, he lived with his mother. They were so poor. They lost their land and their house, and they lived in the hull of a boat that was turned upside down beside the river.

Jack's mother was starting to see signs of winter.

And she was angry. She was facing winter again without food and clothes and a decent shelter. She went over to the door in the hull of the boat, and she looked across the road, and there was Jack stretched out with his head back against a tree.

He was sound asleep. *(deep snoring, head down)* *Oooaaaaaah . . . Oooaaaaaah . . . Oooaaaaaah . . .*

And she yelled, *(angry)* "Jack! *WAKE UP!*"

Well, Jack came out of his deep sleep, *(big stretch)* *streeeeeeeeeeeeeeeetched* himself way out, *(long yawn)* and he said, "Yes, Mama, what is it?"

"You come here. *(point down) NOW!*"

Jack walked over, still shaking the sleep off, and he said, *(sort of groggy)* "What is it?"

His mother said, "We're facing winter again, there's no food in the house, there's no money, we don't have a farm anymore, and you're *asleep.*" She said, "Do you realize that *you* are the reason that we are starving to death?" *(frown and glare)*

"Well, Mama, I've never quite thought about it," Jack said. "Aaaaumm. Are we?"

"Yes!" she said. "We've got *one* cow left, and she's such a bag of bones nobody would want her.

"Jack! WAKE UP!"

▬▬▬▬▬▬▬▬▬▬

THE MESSAGES IN STORIES:
As the Jack tales gathered over the years, all kinds of messages were gathered in them. I will use this tale to explain what I mean.

Before that, I'll tell you where the tale came from. A few years ago, I met a storyteller in Scotland who belonged to a group called the Tinkers. These Tinkers had been gypsies, traveling all over tinkering with pottery, you know, fixing people's pots and pans. Well, these Tinkers also gathered the folklore of Scotland, and they became storytellers. Well, this fellow and his friends were taken with the fact that I told Jack tales too. We decided to swap stories. One fellow told me about "Jack's Trip to Hell." I said, "If I give you one of my stories, can I have that one?" He said, "Mine is worth two of yours." And I believe it is.

But I suggest, young man, that you take this cow to town and that you *sell* her. And on the way home, bring me a sack of coffee."

Jack said, "Mama, you know this is a bad time; what if I don't sell the cow?"

"Well," she said, "then don't you come home."

"Yes, ma'am."

So Jack put a rope around the cow, pulled it away from the house, and waved goodbye. For some reason, deep down inside his brain, he felt he would never see his mama again. But off he went.

He stopped people along the way and he said, "I got a nice cow here. Would you like to buy her?"

People looked at the cow. "Is *that* what that is?"

"Oh," Jack said, "she looks puny, but if you feed her good, she'll fill up. Be just like any other cow."

Well, (shrug shoulders) they refused to buy.

Soon Jack was gone from home a whole month. *Nobody* wanted that cow.

But as he walked along, there up on a little hill, he saw a farmstead. It was a beautiful farmstead. Oh my, the buildings, the house, the shed, the barns, everything was painted white with green shutters around the windows.

"Somebody lives here," Jack said.

"And they've got money."

So Jack walked up to the house and he knocked. He could hear footsteps coming from a *looong* ways back in the house. The door opened and there, standing in front of him, was a short little old man.

"...you take this cow to town..."

So Jack takes the family cow to sell because it's the most valuable thing they own. It's the easiest thing to sell too, 'cause everybody needed milk for cooking and for babies, everybody wanted a cow. So Jack had an important task.

Now, the most famous Jack tale is about his trip to the market to sell the cow, and selling it for magic beans. But how many of us have been sent on a big task and came back with something ridiculous? Something nobody can use at all. But it always turns out all right, it turns out better than we might have thought. That's a part of life. And that's your basic Jack story.

"Oh," said the old man. "How do you do, sonny?"

Jack said, "I'm Jack. I've got me a cow to sell."

"Oh," the old man said, "is that right?"

He looked at the cow. "You sure that's a cow? I ain't seen a cow in a long time. I guess I forgot they looked like that," the old man said.

Jack said, "Well, this here ain't your ordinary cow. This one's kinda hungry. But, if you feed this cow, she'll fill up and she'll be a good cow for you."

The old man said, "Son, I'd like to buy your cow, but I don't have any money."

Jack said, "But look at this farm. It's a *fine* farm. All the buildings are in good shape, all painted white, it's a wonderful place."

The old man said, "But I still got no money. *Hah!* I just got plenty of whitewash."

Jack said, "Oh. Well, I thank you just the same."

The man said, "Son, I'd like to help. You know, when I was a boy, my papa would send me out to sell things and I had me a good-luck piece," he said.

"Now I'm old, I ain't gonna live long, and I ain't going to need that good luck. Why don't I just pass it on to you? It will help you sell *(point)* that cow."

Jack said, "Well . . . all right, I'll take it."

From his pocket the old man took a little book. It was about two inches long and about an inch thick.

He handed it to Jack.

Jack said, *(skeptical)* "This is your good luck-piece?"

The old man said, "Yessir, it is."

Jack said, "Well, I don't know how much luck it's gonna bring me, but because you give it to me, I'm gonna keep it." And he put it in his pocket.

"Son, I'd like to help."

Over the years, Jack tales fill with messages, all sorts of messages. Here, Jack finds an old man who provides him with something he will need. It's a kind of magic bean, but Jack doesn't know that yet. The man knows that Jack will have a hard time selling that cow and he provides for him. The man helps Jack on his way.

J ack walked along, and soon, when he was gone for two months, he came up on a crossroad. One road led to the north, another led south. One road led to the east, another led west. He couldn't go back 'cause he hadn't sold that cow.

So he said, "G'bye Mama, I'm not coming home."

And he stepped away from the middle of that crossroad and headed north. But he hadn't walked more than ten steps when he stopped (pause) 'cause he heard something behind him. It sounded like *Shhhhip . . . shhhhip . . . shhhhhhip.*

Now Jack thought, "When I was standing there a few seconds ago, there was nothing there. What is it now that's making noise?" He turned to look.

There, on the very spot he had just stepped away from, was this *huge* boulder. Propped against this boulder was a tall skinny *daaark* man. He had a black suit with a *long* frock tail coat and a tall hat. Had a piece of wood in his hand and a pocketknife.

Shhhhip, (whittle your finger) *shhhhip . . . shhhhhhhip.*

Jack said, "Ahmmm. How are you doin'?"

And the man said, "*Howdy,* Jack. *Hahaaaaaa.*" He *seeeeemed* (puzzled) to know Jack.

Jack said, "Whatcha doing?"

The man said, "I'm whittling on a piece of wood."

Jack said, "I wanna sell this cow. Wanna buy it?"

The man said, "Well, I don't know. It depends. What would the cow cost me?"

Jack said, "I'll take anything for her. *Anything.*"

The man said, "Well, I might just have anything. *Hahaaa.*" He opened his coat and took out his purse, a purse that was *waaay* too big to fit inside the coat.

"He SEEEEEMED to know Jack."

Uh oh. The crossroads, that's where you meet the Devil, that's where the Devil stands. That's where he can be found any time, in any folklore, that's where you go to find him. Whittling 'cause he has lots of leisure, he has nothing to do. He's just idle, the idle mind is the Devil's workshop.

But Jack didn't think about things like that.

Things didn't lay on Jack's mind too long, and he watched as the man handed the purse to him.

Jack took it and said, "Thank ya. What's in it?"

"Open it and see if that's the price of your cow."

Jack opened the purse. Way down deep inside the purse *(look way down)* was a big pile of *gold coins*.

And he said, "This is what you're gonna give me for the price of this old bag of . . . for this cow?"

The man said, "If that's what you think the cow is worth, *(lean forward and stare)* you take the coins."

Jack began to stuff gold coins into his pocket, and when the purse was empty, he snapped it shut. He gave it back to the man, but as he gave it back, he heard something *jingling* inside the purse.

Jack said, "I don't think I got 'em all."

"HOWDY, Jack. HAHAAAAAA."

Oh, I love to tell this story, I love to become these characters. The old man who gave Jack the good-luck piece, he was a good man, a provider. But this one, this one is different, he's crafty and he's much more sinister than a witch.

When he opened the purse again, *hahaaaaaaa!*
It was filled with the same amount of gold coins.
Jack emptied the coins out, put them in his pocket,
and handed the man the purse. But then again
he heard the same jingling inside it.

"Oh, I didn't get 'em all," he said.

The man said, *(sly and crafty)* "Wait a minute, Jack.
Let me save you a little time. That, my friend,
is a purse that's known as *(lean forward)* *fortunachees*.
It's a magic purse. Every time you open it and
remove the coins, it fills up again. It's never empty."

He said, "Jack, why don't you take this purse
and let it give you gold from now on? Will that be
good enough for the price of your cow?"

"*Oooohaaaa*," Jack said. *(happily)*

"No," he said. *(regretful)* "That wouldn't be fair.
This cow is almost dead. She's just a bag of bones.
I can't let you give me this much gold for a cow
that might drop dead right now."

"Well," said the man. "You are an honest man.
I like that, Jack. I'll tell you what, you take the purse
and enjoy that gold. One of these days, when I think
you have the cost of the purse, then I'll come and
I'll take it. You'll have paid me back."

"Yes," Jack said, *(thrilled)* "I'll become a rich man.
I'll buy everything I can buy, and then you can come
and choose what you want for the price of this purse.

"*Ooooooh*," Jack said. "Yes, yes."

The man said, "Yes, Jack, that sounds about right."

Jack said, "Thank you, thank you so much.
Here's your cow, hmhmm. But don't you want me
to tell you where I'm going to live?"

"When he opened the purse . . ."

Ah, the magic purse, the golden goose, the big temptation. Jack is selling more than a cow here, but the temptation is too great. Anything that can hatch gold can stir up a lot of greed, just like the Haints did in "Soldier Jack." It's hard to resist gold for an old bag-of-bones cow, and that's a fact.

And the man said, "*I know* where you live, Jack."

Jack said, "Okay. Okay." And he started home.

And as he walked away from the man, he thought he heard the man say, *(evil, evil laugh)*

*Whooo**hoooohaaaaa**aaaaaaaaaeeeeeeeeeeeeeee.*

He just wasn't sure. *(quietly with a frown)*

Before Jack returned home, he bought his mama a coffee farm in Peru, so she would never be without coffee again. Then he bought a house for every day of the week, and a castle for the weekend. And in every room in every house and in the castle too, there was a fresh pot of coffee brewing at all times of the day.

He also had herds of cattle and flocks of sheep.

"WHOOOHOOOOHAAAAAA..."

And he had horses, the *finest* horses you ever did see.

And he had fields of corn and wheat and barley.

Jack was a rich man. Jack's mother was so happy with Jack, oh, they had the *best* time.

But you know, *(sad pause)* Jack was a lonely man.

He had his mama and his farm and his animals, but he needed companionship. And the only woman that Jack saw that he liked was the King's daughter.

And the King's daughter liked Jack.

Well, finally Jack got up the nerve to ask the King if he could marry his daughter.

And the King agreed.

The King invited 5,000 people to the wedding.

Soon it was Jack's wedding day. He got up early, and he was so nervous he didn't know what to do. He walked back and forth and back and forth.

His mama said, "Jack, *whatever* is the matter?"

"Mama, I'm so nervous I don't know what to do. I finally met the woman of my dreams, and we are going to marry today. I'm excited and I'm nervous."

She said, "Have a cup of coffee. That'll help ya."

"Oh, Mama, no," he said. "I'll tell you how I'm going to calm myself down. I'm gonna saddle up my finest horse and ride through the corn."

"Jack," she said, "that's a good idea, you do that. But don't you mess up your wedding suit."

Jack said, "If I do, you can clean it up for me."

"I'll be glad to," she said, "and while I'm cleaning your suit, you can drink that cup of coffee."

Jack said, *(happy nod)* "Yes, ma'am."

Jack got on his horse and rode through the corn. He liked to ride early in the morning, the corn smelled so sweet, and he liked to feel the cold drops

"Jack's mother was so happy . . ."

━━━━━━━━━━━━━━

So Jack doesn't sell the cow for something ridiculous, he brings back lots of gold. So the family won't starve, and Jack's mother has her never-ending supply of coffee, with a pot in every room. You see, when these stories were gathered, coffee was not easy to come by, and anybody who had that much coffee was a very rich person. Most people could afford only a nickel sack at a time.

"And the King's daughter . . ."

━━━━━━━━━━━━━━

Yes, always the King's daughter. In the Jack tales, that was the best thing, that was the big prize. If he married the King's daughter, Jack could live happily ever after.

of the fresh dew on his hands and his face.

But as Jack was riding in the corn, something hit him in the shoulder, something hit him so hard, it knocked him facedown between the rows of corn.

Jack said, *(furious)* "*That* makes me mad."

Jack said, "I have *told* people about their children chunking rocks at me. Now, that is *it*. I'm gonna find them young'ns, and *(punch hand)* I'm gonna whomp 'em.

"That's what I'm gonna do."

But Jack didn't seem to be able to get up. Whatever hit him knocked him *square* off that horse. He pushed and he pushed, but he couldn't get up.

Jack said, "I'm weak, what has happened to me?" And then he heard a voice above his head.

"Get up, Jack, *(look down)* get up now! GET UP!"

"...what has happened to me?"

Jack said, "Whoever you are, you gotta help me.

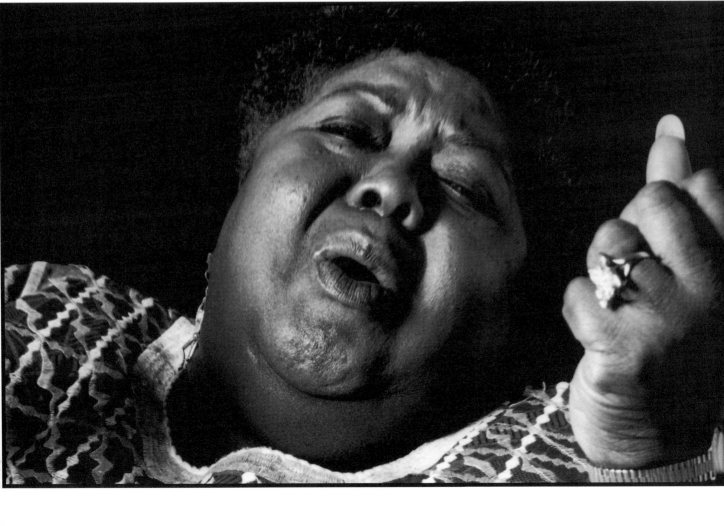

I'm too weak to get up, them children bumped me off my horse with their chunking rocks. *Help me.*"

"*GET UP, JACK,* *(loud and harsh)* ***GET UP!***"

Jack said, "Do you not hear me trying to tell you to give me some help?" Then Jack pushed himself up to his knees. And when he got to his knees he saw who it was. It was *(gulp, eyes wide)* the same man who had given him the hatching purse.

Jack said, *(amazed)* "It's you, it's *you*, my good friend. I'm glad to see ya," Jack said, "I'm glad to see ya."

The man said, *(mocking)* "I'm glad to be here, Jack."

Jack said, "Did my mama tell you where I was?"

The man said, "No, she didn't."

"Oh," Jack said, "I told her anytime I was away and you came by, she was to lay out all my property, and you could pick whatever you want.

"How did you know I was here?" Jack said.

"I told you, Jack, I *always* know where you are."

"Oh," Jack said, "this is wonderful. You know, this is my wedding day. And I don't have a daddy. So I'd like to have somebody stand up for me. Would you do that? Would you be my best man?"

And the man said, "Haah! I *am* the best man."

"That's what I said, that's what I said," Jack said. "Now I've done met the woman of my dreams. I'm getting ready to live and be happy," Jack said. "And I'm just so happy that you came by."

Jack said, "After the wedding, me and my bride and you can go back to the house, and I will lay out everything I own. You'll be *surprised* at what I own. You can choose *(spread arms)* anything you want."

"Oh," the man said, *(mocking again)* "that's nice, Jack.

"And I'm just so happy that . . ."

Jack's a little dense here, but you know, the point of the whole tale, Jack's big surprise, is just about to come, so I like to really stretch it out, I like to keep 'em waiting.

But you see, I already *have* what I want," he said.

"Ooooh," Jack said. "You're way ahead of me. What did you choose? You didn't choose my bride, did you? *(giggle)* He*heeeeeee*."

"No, Jack," the man said. "Look down."

And Jack looked down.

"Well, look at that," Jack said. "There's a man spread out there between the rows of corn. Got on a suit just like mine. Them young'ns chunking rocks knocked him off his horse, just like me."

The man said, "Look again, Jack."

Jack said, "*Oooh, (eyes very big) that's MEEE*."

The man said, "That's right, Jack."

Jack said, *(very puzzled)* "What's wrong with me? Wait a minute. If that's me, *(pluck at yourself)* who's *this?*"

"Jack, down there is your *body*," the man said.

"If that's me, who's THIS?"

"Now, *(point at the listener)* this here is your *soul*."

Jack said, *(howl)* "*Nooooo.* That means I'm *DEAD.*"

The man said, "*Hahaaaah.* That's right."

Jack said, "But wait, how do I explain to Mama that I dropped dead on my wedding day? *(whimpering)*

"And how do I explain that to my bride?"

"No explanation needed. They will understand."

"But just let me tell Mama that I won't be back. Let me explain to my bride that I'm dead."

The man said, "I've got a long way to go, Jack, and you're going with me. I can't let you go back."

Jack said, *(baffled)* "Who *are* you?"

The man said, "Some call me *HELLZABAH.*

"Some folks call me *(pop eyes wide open)* *LUUUCIFER.*

"And other folks call me *(long hiss)* *SSSSSATAN.*

"But I just *love* to be called *DEVIL. Haaaah!*"

"Some call me HELLZABAH."

Just like ghosts in scary stories, the Devil in Jack tales is always interesting. He's crafty, and kids love to hate him just as much as they love to hate mean witches. So you have to get the Devil right too, you have to feel like him and look sneaky and evil like he does. You can have lots of fun with the Devil, if you just let yourself go.

Jack said, "Oooo, you're the Devil? But, Devil, what do you want with *meeeeee?*"

The Devil said, *(quietly)* "Don't you remember, Jack? You took a purse, a purse that gives everlasting gold. A purse that's never empty. I have to be paid for it."

Jack said, "But I have *things.* Things to give you."

The Devil said, "Things? I have my own things. I needed another soul, and now I have yours."

Jack said, "Please, *(plead) please* don't take my soul. Let me have my soul."

But the Devil said, "Jack, I'm taking you to hell."

Jack pleaded and begged all the way to the gates of hell. When they stopped in front of the gates, the Devil took his keys, looking for just the right one.

"Listen, Jack, I'm going to take you in here. You'll see a bunch of folks who're already confused. I'll not have you beggin' and pleadin' like this.

"So you *(point) keep your mouth SHUT!*"

Then the Devil put the key in the door, *(twist hand)* unlocked the gates of hell, and drug Jack inside.

It was a sight that Jack had never seen before.

People were working *(point one way)* on this side.

People were working *(point other way)* on that side.

People were working up here and down here, and people were working over there.

Jack said, "You know, I didn't work too much while I was on earth. Do I have to work here?"

The Devil said, "*Hm.* I got a special job for you."

Jack said, *(roll eyes)* "I thought maybe you did."

The Devil kept walking. He took Jack down into the inner sanctum of hell. It was very *daaaark.*

When he opened the door, you have never heard

"... PLEASE don't take my soul."

We haven't reached the pinnacle of the story yet, but here is where the story turns. Your soul is your most valuable treasure. If you control your soul, if you can keep it intact and not sell it, then you have done a tremendous thing, you get into heaven and you will be happy. But we often end up giving our souls to the Devil, even when we know we're doing it. You have to watch out, watch out all the time. Jack was afraid when he realized what he'd done, and begged to get his soul back. But he would have to fight for it.

so much noise in all your life. There was screaming and hollering and cursing in the pitch black dark.

Jack said, "Don't leave me, don't leave me. Where am I? *(panicky) Please help me.*"

The Devil said, "This here's my special room."

Jack said, "Who's making all that noise in here?"

"Let me put a little light on the subject," the Devil said. He went to the middle of the room, opened a furnace door, and light *flooded* the room.

Jack could see shelves upon shelves upon shelves of little cages. And inside all of those little cages were little tiny things with great big old heads. Little bodies with long *long* arms and great big hands on them too, *(wiggle fingers)* with long skinny fingers.

Jack said, *"Baaaaaaaaaah. What's that?"*

The Devil said, *(proud and wicked)* "Them's my Imps."

"Jack could see shelves . . . "
"Baaaaaaaaaaah. What's that?"

Oh boy, the Devil's Imps. I used to think they were cream-colored when I first heard the story in Scotland, I could see them sort of creamy, but now I think that Imps have no color at all. They're just out-and-out ugly without color.

Jack said, "Imps? I heard of them things, but I ain't never seen 'em before. *(lean back)* They's *ugly*."

The Devil said, "I think they's very cute myself."

Jack said, *(frown)* "What do you do with an Imp?"

The Devil smiled and he said, *(snicker)* "*Heheeeee*, I send them out on earth to keep up hell."

"Ooh," Jack said, "what kinda hell d'you mean?"

"Well," the Devil said. "Let me tell you.

"This bunch over here breaks up marriages.

"This bunch over here knows how to start wars.

"This bunch's got 75 different kinds of religions.

"And that bunch over there, *haaaaaah!* Well, they's got all kinds of stuff to put in your mind, change your brain waves, *hoohaaaaa*."

"Well," Jack said, "but, Devil, why am I in here? What am I gonna do with Imps?"

"Mmmmm," the Devil said. "Well, you see all them Imp fingers on the end of all them Imp hands? You see what they're doing with them?"

The Imps were sticking fingers through the bars of the cages and *(twist fingers)* picking at the locks.

The Devil said, "They can take them Imp fingers and pick the locks. And when they get the locks off, they come out of the cages. Run all over the place, they do, and they lose weight, and they get tired. Then, when I get ready to send them out on earth, they're too tired to keep up hell."

The Devil said, "Now, Jack, your job is gonna be to keep 'em from breaking them locks."

Jack said, *(frown)* "How would I do that?"

The Devil said, "Here, I'll show you."

He picked up his walking cane, spotted an Imp

"What do you do with an Imp?"

You see, Imps must be colorless because they take on the color and personality of the people they're sent into. That's why they're sent, you know, to keep up hell, to cause the world's troubles. So they might look like Fidel Castro or our President, or like all those guys in politics. Yeah, whether good or really bad, they've all got some Imp in 'em.

that had the lock open, took the cane and hit it.

"*Get on back in there!*" he said. "*GET BACK!* If you don't get back there, (swing arm) I'll ram this thing right down your throat. *GET BACK!*"

And the Imp looked down at the Devil.

"*BAAH! ShabalapSHABAlapSHABALAP!*"

Jack said, (pop eyes) "Did you hear that? That was the meanest, ugliest thing I've ever heard in my life."

The Devil said, "Yes, I taught him how to curse like that, mmm, uh huh. Wasn't that cute?"

Jack said, "Noo*oooooooo*."

The Devil said, "Wait, wait. Here's another one. Watch this. *Get BACK!* Go ahead now, get *BACK!* If you don't get back, I'll knock you out! *Get back!*"

The Imp looked at the devil and said,

"*ShabalapSHABAlapSHABAlapSHABALAP!*

"GET ON BACK IN THERE!"

"SHABADALAPshagabaBAMshagabaBAM!"

Jack said, "That was worse than the other one."

The Devil said, "Ha*haaaa*. I taught him too."

Jack said, "What am I supposed to do?"

The Devil said, "Here, see that one up there?
He's got his Imp fingers out. *(point up)* *Go get him*."

Jack took the walking cane and went to the cage.
He said, *(very timid)* "Little fellow, you there, g-g-go back.
You mustn't do that. Go on now."

The Imp looked at Jack. "*Whaaaaaaaaa!*
"*BAAH! ShabalapSHABALAPlaplapLAP!*"

Jack said, "Oh *no*. *(cover eyes)* Nobody has *ever* said
a thing like that to me. Oh, that was *HORRIBLE!*"

"Now, listen," the Devil said. "I've got to be gone
for 100 years," he said. "When I get back here,
I better be able to count *every* one of them Imps,

"Oh, that was HORRIBLE!"

▬▬▬▬▬▬▬▬▬▬▬

Well, you know, not everybody has seen an Imp, and I really have to give them a good picture, I have to let them know about all that cursing. Hah! I love all that.

Now, remember that I said you should never, never memorize a story, and this cursing is a good example of what I mean. Just let yourself go, don't worry about doing it the same way every time, make the angriest sounds that you can. One man came up to me one night with a big piece of paper in his hand and said, "Now, that cursing, could you spell that for me?" Well, I just couldn't.

and they better be fat and sassy and ready to go."

Jack said, "But how many do you have in here?"

"Last count, I had 100 million," the Devil said.
"And they better be here *(clap hands)* when I get back."

And he disappeared.

Well, all Jack could do was look around. Then, when Jack started into his job, the Imps started right into Jack. They tore his clothes until he was naked; he had nothing but a belt and pockets hanging off it.

He had three hairs left on his head,

he had two teeth in his mouth,

his ears were hanging down on his shoulders,

his eyes wouldn't stay in their sockets,

and he had two toes left on his feet.

The Imps spat on him, they slapped him, and they scratched him. For 40 years Jack ran around trying to keep them Imps in their cages.

He just couldn't take it anymore.

He said, "I don't care *what* the Devil does to me. I can't stand this. I've got to do something."

Suddenly *(look down)* he felt something in his pocket.

He dug down deep.

"Look here," he said. "It's my good-luck piece. I don't care what the Devil does, I can't stand it. I'm gonna read this here book. Maybe it'll keep me from getting spit on and scratched."

So Jack took the book to the light of the furnace.

He pushed one eye back into its socket, *(push eye)*

put his ear on upside down, *(twist ear)*

and commenced to read the book. *(hold hand up)*

"And he opened the bibble."

You see, Jack was illiterate and he was doing the best he could. He thought he was reading from the bibble. I mean, if your eyeball is hanging out on your shirt, you know you're seeing double. But still, I leave it to the imagination of the listener to see what I'm describing, and to understand all these weird things. Because the sights of hell are not seen, the imagination will probably create a hell which is much worse than what I say. That's why I want your mind to work on what I say.

"Bee-eye-bee-ell-eee. *(frown)* *Bibble*."

And he *(unfold hands)* opened the bibble.

"*In the beeeginning . . . was the word*," he read.

"*And . . . the word was God.* (nod and smile)

"*And the word . . . was with God.*" (nod and nod)

Suddenly Jack noticed it was quiet in the room. He looked all around. Sure enough, the Imps were caught in midair listening to Jack. Some of 'em were still holding the locks, but they were all listening.

"*And the word was . . . without form or . . . void.*

"*And God said . . . let there be light.*" (look around)

The Imps were still listening. *(look around again)*

So Jack said, *(loud)* "Did you all like that?"

And the Imps said *(nod and nod and nod)*

Jack said, "Wouldya like me to read some more?"

And the Imps said *(nod more quickly)*

Jack said, "If I read to you, will you sit still? And not spit on me and scratch me and carry on?"

And they said *(shake head, no, no, no)*

Jack said, "All right then, I'm gonna read to you. But I'm gonna watchya, now." *(look suspicious)*

"*In . . . the beeeginning,* (look up quick and down)

"*God created the heaven and the earth.*"

Jack noticed that in the cages way in the back the Imps were holding their skinny Imp fingers behind their ears like they couldn't hear too well.

So Jack said, *(louder)* "Can you *HEAR* back there?"

And the Imps said *(shake head no, no, no)*

Jack said, "Wouldya like to get out of the cages?"

And the Imps said *(nod and nod, yes)*

Jack said, "Well, wait a minute." And it took Jack 20 years to go around and empty all those cages.

"The Imps were still listening."

They don't say anything, they just nod a lot. Jack's good-luck piece finally pays off for him, and its magic holds the Imps still. The point is clear, but I don't say that, I don't say anything about that at all. If I have brought you into the story, the image you have of the scene does everything you need.

Then he *rowed* the Imps up, all in a line.

Jack said, "Now, don't touch one another!"

And they didn't. *(squeeze one way and another way)*

Jack said, "Put them Imp fingers in your lap!"

And they did. *(put fingers in lap)*

And Jack read. And he read. And he read.

Well, it took Jack as *long* as it took him to read to the Imps. They never moved and they all listened.

On the very last day, when Jack finished reading the bibble and closed it, the Devil popped in.

"*Hah! (clap hands)* I'm *baaaaaaaaack!*" he said.

"Wait, why is it so quiet in here? What's wrong?"

Jack said, *(worried)* "Ain't nothing wrong."

"Yes there is. This room's supposed to be *wild*," the Devil said. *(angry)* "I'm supposed to hear cursin'.

"Wait, why is it so quiet in here?"

"It's quiet in here. *WHERE ARE MY IMPS?*"

"They're here," Jack said. "Look down here."

The Devil looked down, and he couldn't believe what he saw. All the Imps were just looking up.

The Devil said, *"These? THESE are my Imps?"*

The Imps were all looking (goofy smile) at the Devil.

"What's *wrong* with them?" the Devil said. "They's all glazed over or something."

"They're all right, they're all right," Jack said. "I've just been reading to them. That's all, *reading.*"

The Devil said, "Reading? *Reading to Imps?* You don't *READ* to Imps. What were you reading?"

Jack said, "I was reading this bibble." (hold up hand)

The Devil said, "What's a *bibble?* Let me see it."

He snatched the book from Jack's hand and he held it up to the light of the furnace.

"This ain't no bibble, this is a *BIBLE,*" he said. *"You've done CONVERTED 100 million Imps."*

Well, the Devil, *he was mad.*

The Devil was so mad he threw Jack out of hell. And 100 million Imps with him. Jack had so many Imps he didn't know what to do with them. So he took some north, he took some south, he took some east and west, and they repopulated the earth.

Now, listen.

If you get to yellin' at your children,
or hollerin' at your husband,
or screamin' at your neighbor,
don't feel bad, you can't help yourself.

You are a direct descendent from those Imps that were thrown out of hell with Jack.

. . . And *that's* the end of *that.*

Br'er Tales

BR'ER TALES

This is Grandpa's cane. It's not much of a cane, is it? It's just so lightweight. But he was a little fellow and he had arthritis. I suppose the cane was just to keep him from stumbling. But I remember when the cane seemed heavier, I remember holding on to it. When he died, I walked into his house and the bed was gone, his room was empty, and there was nothing hanging on the wall but this walking stick. I knew he couldn't be far because he never went far without his cane. But Grandma said, "He's gone. He's gone to heaven." I thought, "Surely he'll be back, Grandpa can't walk without his walking cane." But you see, he never did come back, and I've got the cane.

We used to walk up the road to Aunt Sally's house to get coffee and cookies. Grandpa used the cane to point out things to me. "Do you see that?" he'd say. I'd say, "See what?" "That! That! *That!*" And sometimes he'd pick up something on the end of it. Like a snake. And I'd say, "Grandpa, put that down." He'd say, "You know what kind of snake this is?" And I'd say, "Yeah, it's a big snake." And then sometimes he'd use his cane to point out a rabbit that had just run across the road and into the woods. "Now, there goes old Br'er Rabbit today." And I'd say, "Oh, Grandpa, that wasn't Br'er Rabbit." "Yes it was," he'd say. "But, Grandpa, how do you know?" And he'd say, "I recognize Br'er Rabbit every time I see him." I'd say, "But that rabbit was brown. The one we saw yesterday was gray. You said *he* was Br'er Rabbit." Well, he looked at me, took the end of his walking cane and put it on my nose, and he said, "You change your clothes, don't you?" Well, I was convinced that Br'er Rabbit really lived 'cause he changed his clothes.

Br'er tales were a big part of my growing up. They were not Uncle Remus tales like most people think; you're not going to find some of them in books at all because Granddaddy told me what his father told him. They're just Br'er Rabbit tales and they are passed from family to family. I didn't know about Uncle Remus and his Br'er tales until I went to the first grade. You see, Uncle Remus was actually a composite of three old men who had once been slaves. They lived on a plantation owned by the grandmother of a little boy

When I tell the Br'er tales, I like to wear these African clothes, they make me feel real good. They're made by hand-weaving strips of cloth and sewing them together. The women paint the patterns in urine, then the cloth strips are dyed. The black in this one is dyed with pure mud. Each region of Africa has its own designs and colors; I have one with paintings of animals that I really like a lot.

named Joel Chandler Harris. She gave the old men a place to stay and took care of them because they didn't have anywhere to go.

Now, Joel Chandler Harris had rheumatic fever, and the doctor said he couldn't go out and play. He had to stay in his bed all the time. But of course, he was only nine years old, and these old men would watch him slip out of the house to play with the other children. So they would stop him. They would keep him in their huts and tell him stories till his mother came to look for him and take him back in the house. But the little boy remembered the stories. Later, when he was 15 years old, he went to Atlanta to become a printer's apprentice. The printer asked him to write a filler for the *Atlanta Constitution*, and that's when he invented the storyteller Uncle Remus, told his first Br'er tale, and began compiling the stories in a book.

Once, when Franklin Roosevelt was traveling through Georgia, he said, "I would like to meet the man who wrote all those colored stories." Joel Chandler Harris was a shy man, but he was brought to

"This is Grandpa's cane . . ."

the President by a black man driver, who got off the wagon and stood beside him. Somebody said to Mr. Roosevelt, "That's Joel Chandler Harris, right over there." And the President walked to the black man and put his hand out, not knowing. Because the stories were so natural, you know, he thought a black man must have written them. Poor Mr. Harris, they say he was just so embarrassed.

Just like me, Joel Chandler Harris was only passing on the stories he had been told by others when he was a child. But my Br'er tales didn't begin with Uncle Remus, you know; it's even hard for me to say Uncle Remus because I didn't know about him. You see, I knew my granddaddy, I knew the fellow himself.

N ow, Br'er Dog, Br'er Raccoon, Sis Goose, Sis Cow, Br'er Wolf, Br'er Bat, and every critter you could think of would slip up to the fence and look up at the man's house. They would watch the man comin' in and out of his house, see him *(throw hands)* throwin' dishwater out the back door, see him throwin' bones out to the critters. And all the critters said,

"We'd like to live in a house like the man."

So one day they kinda suggested to Br'er Rabbit that they had been thinking about *everybody* gettin' together and buildin' a big house like the man had.

Br'er Rabbit said, "That sounds good."

Br'er Rabbit said, "You know, I've always wanted to get out of that tree hole that I've been living in. Hahaaaaaaa*aaaaaaaa*."

"Well, let's do it," said ol' Br'er Raccoon.

So everybody settled down and they talked about what all they would build. Some of them decided to build the walls, others was gonna build the floors and put the windows in, and Br'er Rabbit, he was just sitting there listening.

Then, when everybody had something to build, they said, "Br'er Rabbit, what are you gonna do?"

Br'er Rabbit said, "Well, you know, I don't know. I was thinking I could help you put the walls up. But when I look up too high *(look up)* I get *nervous*."

"Oh," they said. "We don't want you nervous. Don't you build the walls, Br'er Rabbit."

"We'd like to live in a house..."

PARABLES AND ALLEGORIES: Br'er tales are reflections of us. The man lived in a house and the critters watched him, they could tell he was havin' a good time. They lived in hatches and holes, and maybe a house would be real nice. They always wanted what the man had, they gardened and farmed like him, and naturally they wanted to live like he did.

When my mother came down to visit from Chicago, she was just like another little kid for me. She taught me how to make mud pies and cakes, even make the icing, and sometimes we would build a little house out of twigs. When my grandpa would say, "Whatchu been doin', gal?" I'd say, "I built a house with Mama this morning." He'd say, "You did? I bet you it's a fine house. Anything like that house Br'er Rabbit built?" And I knew It was time for a story. I'd sort of settle down close to him, and off he'd go with a Br'er tale.

"Well," Br'er Rabbit said. "Then I was thinkin' of helpin' you put the roof on the house. But when I stands way high like that, my stomach gets jittery."

"Oh," they said. "We don't want your stomach to get jittery. Don't you fool with that."

"Well," Br'er Rabbit said. "I was thinkin' about helpin' put the chimney on top of the house. But you know, when I get to liftin' heavy stuff like that, m'bones ache *(squint)* somethin' awful."

And they said, "You better not lift them bricks. You just do whatever it is you can do."

Br'er Rabbit said, "I'll do that."

Br'er Rabbit went home and got himself a ruler and a pencil. Everybody else was hammerin' and nailin' and carryin' wood, and puttin' in windows, and Br'er Rabbit was *(hand motions)* measurin' and markin',

". . . and Br'er Rabbit was measurin' and markin' . . ."

Br'er Rabbit wanted that house more than the other critters did, but he didn't want to work hard or anything else, so he pretended he was doing all the measurin' and markin'. He didn't really do anything, but he worked so hard at it, they gave him first choice.

measurin' and markin', measurin' and markin', markin' and measurin', measurin' and markin', markin' and measurin'. Doing absolutely nothing but measurin' and markin'.

All the critters watched him run outside and measure something, run inside and mark something.

"Ahhh," they said, "look at Br'er Rabbit. He's just a-measurin' and a-markin'. My, if it weren't for him, we wouldn't know what to do."

Well, soon the house was finished.

The critters all stood back and looked up at it.

It was beautiful.

It was finer than the man's house. The critters were proud of themselves. Now everybody said,

"Which of us is gonna live where in the house? Seein' as how Br'er Rabbit worked harder than anybody else, why don't we give him first choice?"

Br'er Rabbit stepped up with his ruler and pencil in his hand, and he said,

"I do declare I appreciate that. I think I'm gonna take the first room *(point up)* at the top of the steps."

So they said, "It's yours."

And the rest of the critters kinda fell into place throughout the house.

Well. Br'er Rabbit set out to furnish his room.

The first thing he carried up the steps was a great big *(arms wide)* shotgun. He hung it on the wall.

The second thing he put in his room was a huge *(arms wider)* brass cannon. He hid that in a closet.

The third thing he carried up was a #2 tin tub of water. It was heavy, but he got it up the steps.

Well, that night all the critters collected food,

and they had a banquet that was fit for a king.

They were all eating and singing and talking.

"Oh, this is so wonderful," Sis Goose said. "I always wanted to live in an inside pond."

"Oh, this is so nice," said Sis Cow. "I don't have to get wet no more, standing outside in that pasture."

They were having *(shake head)* a wonderful time.

Now, while the critters were talking and talking about how much this house was gonna mean to 'em, Br'er Rabbit was sitting at the end of the table, and he was yawnin' and gappin'.

Eeeeeeeeee*(stretch, huge yawn)*RRRRRRrrrrrrrrrrrr.

Br'er Bear said, "Br'er Rabbit, that's awfully impolite of you. What in the world is *wrong?*"

And Br'er Rabbit said, "It was really hard on me building this here house, and I'm a little tired."

"...he was yawnin' and gappin'."

I didn't need to build twig houses for Grandpa to think of this story, he could just catch me yawning. Anything, any excuse, was always enough for a story; you'd say or do a thing and he'd start right in.

They said, "Well, we're gonna be up for a while 'cause we think we gonna cut a rug in the next room. Why don't you just go to bed?" *(point up)*

Br'er Rabbit said, "I think that's a good idea. I'm gonna say good night to y'all."

And everybody said good night to Br'er Rabbit, and up the stairs he went. Slammed his door.

Well, all the critters started talking again.

Ol' Br'er Hound Dog said, "I can sit on my porch and I can howl all I want to. *Haaaoooowwwwwlllllll. Haaaoooowwwwwlllllll.* Have a good time."

Well, Br'er Rabbit stepped out of his room, cocked that shotgun, and hollered down the steps,

"*When a BIG MAN LIKE ME needs to sit down, WHERE do you reckon he ought to SIT?*"

Well, the critters looked at each other.

They said, "Now, what in the world is wrong with Br'er Rabbit? Why can't he sit down?"

Sis Cow said, *(frown)* "*BIG MAN or LITTLE MAN, SIT WHERE YOU CAN.*"

Br'er Rabbit said, "Look out, I'm gettin' ready to sit down," and he pulled the trigger on that gun.

BOOOOO*OOOOOOOOMMMMMM!*

Well, it shook all the windows, and it knocked Sis Goose right off the chair she was sittin' on.

"Well," Ol' Br'er Raccoon said. "Br'er Rabbit's bigger than I thought he was. When he sits down, he shakes the *whole* house."

"*Fsssshhhuuuuuu,* he's *big!*"

Then they forgot about Br'er Rabbit and started talkin' again about their fine house.

"Don't you like these shinin' new floors? If we

Oh, I love those big noises. This story depends on them; sounds bring kids into the scenes so they can understand what's going on.

You see, the Br'er tales are just adventures that animals have; the dumb ones get themselves in trouble, and the good ones lift them out. They are just like our own adventures. We have good people, we've got sort of dumb people, and we have tricksters. Bugs Bunny is the Disney version of Br'er Rabbit; he's very clever and he has a big sense of humor. Pogo in those Walt Kelly stories is also a possum and he's just as kindhearted as Br'er Possum, he is forever nice and he doesn't really want to trick anybody.

put a little sand on them, ya know, and rub 'em down, they'll be just beautiful."

Br'er Rabbit opened the closet door in his room, pulled that cannon out of the closet, and held the fire over the trigger. Hollered down the steps,

"*When a big man like me NEEDS TO SNEEZE, WHERE do you reckon he ought to SNEEZE?*"

Well, the critters looked at each other again.

"What is *wrong* with him? Whoooooeeeee."

Br'er Hound Dog said, "Big man or little man, *SNEEZE where you PLEASE!*"

Br'er Rabbit said, "Look out down there, I am getting ready to sneeze." And he lifted that cannon.

BOOOOOOOWHAAAMMMMM!

Knocked Br'er Bear (clap hands) right off his chair. He got up and he shook himself and he said,

"SNEEZE where you PLEASE!"

"Br'er Rabbit's got a powerful cold. I don't think I wanna catch it. *(worried)* I'm gonna go out for a while."

Well, everybody was just "*What in the world . . .*"

They didn't realize that Br'er Rabbit was as big as he was. Why, when he sneezed, he broke some of the glass up in the windows and shook the plates off the shelves. "*Fsshhuuuuuuu*, he's somethin'."

They forgot about him. Started talking about how beautiful the walls were, how they were going to add more paint to the walls. It was gonna be nice.

Br'er Rabbit pushed *(hard struggle)* that #2 tin tub full of water over to the top of the stairs.

He hollered down the steps, *(hands around mouth)*

"*When a BIG MAN like me needs a CHEWWW of tobacco, where d'you reckon he ought to SPIT?*"

"BOOOOOOOWHAAAMMMMM!" The critters commenced to lookin' at each other.

"Well, wherever Br'er Rabbit spits," they thought, "I ain't gonna be here when it comes down."

And Br'er Rabbit said, *"LOOK OUT THERE! I'M GETTIN' READY TO SPIT."*

He turned that tub over, and that water came ***KUSSHHHHLOOOOOOSHHHHHHHH!*** Down the steps.

When the critters heard that, they all jumped out the windows and doors, made a coupla new windows and doors, and when the water hit the floor, there wasn't a single critter left.

Then Br'er Rabbit locked the house all up. Nobody ever came back.

But Br'er Rabbit lived there till the day he died.

. . . And *that's* the end of that.

"LOOK OUT THERE!"

Once, when I said I wanted to tell an Uncle Remus tale, the school principal said he'd rather I didn't. He said, "We're trying to teach these children pride." But I think Br'er tales teach values in ways that preaching never can. "You don't have pride unless you know where you came from," I said.

BR'ER POSSUM'S DILEMMA

Y ou know, years ago when all the critters could talk and walk like you and me, there lived a fellow named Br'er Possum. And *ooooooooold* Br'er Possum, well, he was a kindhearted, quiet little old fellow.

Liked to hang upside down in the tree, you know, hang by his tail *(raise hooked finger)* to sleep at night.

Well, sir, ol' Br'er Possum, he would come down out of that tree, and he'd walk along the road searching for stuff to eat. Specially if he had been in the 'simmon tree. Oh, he liked green 'simmons.

Ol' Br'er Possum would walk along his way, and any time you saw him he'd be grinnin' at ya.

Haa*haaaaaa.*

Well, one day Br'er Possum was walking along, and he come up on a *greeeeeeat* big old hole in the middle of the road. Instead of Br'er Possum just goin' on down the road minding his business, he stopped *(pause)* and looked *(look down)* in that hole.

Well, when he looked down, he jumped back.

'Cause layin' down in the bottom of that hole was ol' Br'er Snake. *(snaky motions)*

And ol' Br'er Snake had a *brick* on his back.

Br'er Possum said, "I best get on outta here. Br'er Snake is mean and evil, low-down and *sneaky.*"

Br'er Possum backed up from the hole and went on down the road. But unbeknownst to him, Br'er Snake had already seen him.

Br'er Snake had put that brick on his own back

"Well, when he looked down ..."

DIALECTS AND ODD SOUNDS: *Snake or possum, both would be called Br'er. "Br'er" is a term for brother or mister; it's southern dialect. Men would speak to one another in church, call somebody Brother Jones, and "Br'er Jones" is the way it sounded. And the white men would often call the older black men "Uncle." It was not derogatory, they were truly, you know, being nice to them.*

My grandma told me this story in the old slave dialect. Both my grandparents spoke wonderful dialect, but I can't. Some of the words are difficult and children wouldn't understand them. So I read the old stories many times, put them in regular English, and then throw in a bit of dialect here and there. Then I explain that the words come from slave dialect. But still, I know my dialect isn't quite right and I try to stay away from it. Even with all the practice in the world, if the dialect you use isn't right, you can ruin the story.

just to get attention. So before Br'er Possum got out of earshot, Br'er Snake commenced to calling him.

"*Heeeeeeelp me.* **(look up)** *Br'er Paaaawwssum.*"

Br'er Possum stopped and he turned to listen.

He said, "That's ol' Br'er Snake a-callin' to me. What you reckon he wants?" Br'er Possum figured, well, as long as Br'er Snake was calling, he wanted to find out what he wanted.

See, Br'er Possum was kindhearted.

He never liked to see nobody in trouble, and he knew Br'er snake was in trouble. He went back to the hole and he stood there. Kinda cautious-like.

He said, "Br'er Snake, aaah, was you calling me?"

Br'er Snake looked up out of that hole, kinda lifted his head, and he said to Br'er Possum,

"*Taaaaaaassssssssssssssssssssss.* **(wiggle tongue, long hiss)**

"'. . . aaah, was you calling me?' Br'er Snake looked up . . ."

Br'er Possum was the kindest of all the critters. He was real good. You can feel how gullible he is, but you know he's going to try to do the right thing. Br'er Snake was tricky and nasty; you should feel that too. That's why I stretch him out. I pause before he talks, stick out my tongue and wiggle it. "Taaassssss." I take time with it and I shake my head a little too. "Taaaaaasssssssssss." Very nasty.

"I've been down here in this hole with this here brick on my back. Won't you help me to get it off?

"*Taaaaaaasssss*ssssssssssssssss." *(wiggle tongue, long hiss)*

Br'er Possum said, "Unh unh."

He said, "Now, listen, Br'er Snake, I know you from old. You're mean, evil, low-down, and sneaky. If I was to commence to get you outta that hole, you wouldn't do nothing but bite me for sure."

And ol' Br'er Snake said,

"*Taaaaaaasssss*ssssssssssssssssssssssss. *(longer hiss)*

"Maybe, maybe not. Maa*aaaaaaaaaybe not.*

"*Taaaaaaasssss*ssssssssssssssss."

Br'er Possum said, "I got to think on this a bit."

Br'er Possum thought high and he thought low. As he was thinking high, he saw an old dead limb hanging out of the tree. So he turned to that tree and he broke that limb, and he dropped it down into the hole, and he pushed that brick off of Br'er Snake's back. Then he threw that limb back and took off down the road.

Boooggiddy boooggiddy boooggiddy boooggiddy.

"Ha*haaaa*," he said. "Hoo*hooooooooooo.* I got away from him that time. *Haaaahaaaaa.*"

And then he heard, "*Heeelp* me, Br'er Pooossum."

Br'er Possum said, *(frown)* "That's him again. I got the brick off his back, what does he want now?"

Br'er Possum didn't know, but he was worried.

He was kindhearted, you see, and never wanted to see anybody in trouble. So he turned around and went back. There in the hole lay ol' Br'er Snake.

Br'er Possum said, "Br'er Snake, was that you callin' to me? What do you want now?"

"I got to think on this a bit."

Oh heavens, is that possum really going to fall for this? I really try to stretch the nasty snake stuff. Oftentimes the length of a story will be the time you have to tell it. So you can add more hissing or you can take some hissing out. But that hissing is important, it's what children think of when they ask you to tell this story again.

And ol' Br'er Snake said,
"*Taaaaaaassss*ssssssssssssssssss*.

I've been down here in this hole for a long time, and I've gotten a little weak. The sides of the hole is just too slick for me. Aah, won't you help me climb out?"

Br'er Possum said, "No*oooo*."

He said, "I *know* you, Br'er Snake. If I was to help you out, *(shake head)* well, you'd bite me for sure."

And ol' Br'er Snake said,
"*Taaaaaaassss*ssssssssssssssssss*.

"Maybe, maybe not. Maaaaa*aaaybe not. Hahaa.
"*Taaaaaaassss*ssssssssssssssssss*."

Br'er Possum said, "Let me think on that a little."

Br'er Possum thought high and he thought low.

As he was thinking low, he happened to see

"Then he threw that limb back . . ." that same branch he broke off and put in the hole.

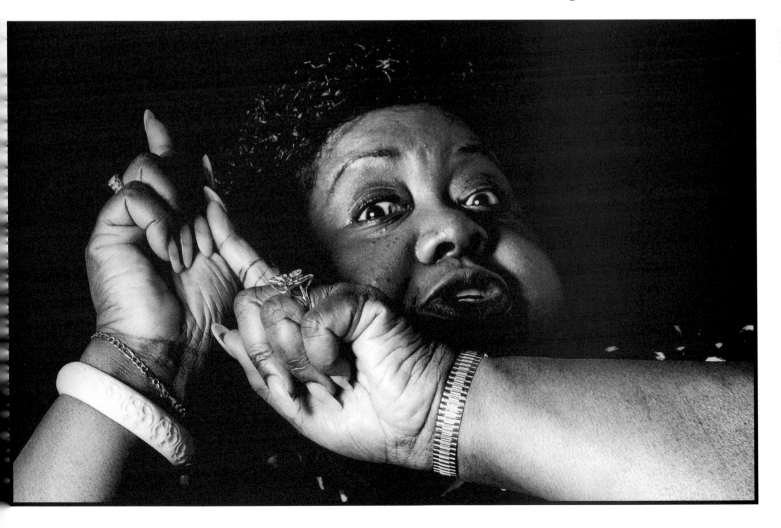

So he picked it up, and he stuck it *waaaaaaay* down beneath ol' Br'er Snake, and he *lifted* Br'er Snake high up into the air, and *(throw arms back)* *threw* him back into the high grass, then he threw that limb down and he took off down the road.

    Boooggiddy boooggiddy boooggiddy boooggiddy.

    "Ha*haaaa*," he said. "Hoo*hoooooooooo.*

I got away from him that time. *Hahah.*"

    "*Help me*, Br'er Possum."

    And Br'er Possum said, "Uh oh. It's him again."

    But you know, Br'er Possum was kindhearted.

    So he turned around and went back to the hole.

He stood there cautious-like, looking for Br'er Snake.

    "Br'er Snake? Ah, Br'er Snake, *where you at?*"

    All of a sudden ol' Br'er Snake come *a-crawling* up out of the high grass. *(snaky motions)*

"HELP ME, Br'er Possum."

He crawled across the road, stretched himself way out, and he said,

"Taaaaaaaassss**ssssssssssssssssss**.
I've been down in that hole for a *mighty* long time; I got a little cold. Could you put me in your pocket and get me warm?

"Taaaaaaaassss**sssssssssssssssssss**."

Br'er Possum said, "Are you *crazy?*

"I done took that brick off your back, took you out of that hole, now you're talkin' about . . . *Noooo,* I know you, Br'er Snake, you're mean and evil, low-down and sneaky. If I put you in my pocket, you wouldn't do nothing but bite me and kill me."

And ol' Br'er Snake said,

"Taaaaaaaassss**sssssssssssssssssssssssssss**. *(longer hiss)*

"Maybe, maybe not. Maaaa*aaaa*ybe *not.*"

"Are you CRAZY?"

In another version of this story, Br'er Possum says, "Oh, I can't understand this Br'er Snake; can we go to Br'er Rabbit and figure it out?" Well, Br'er Snake figures good, that means two meals. But when they tell Br'er Rabbit the problem, he keeps saying, "Now, wait a minute. You say you were where?" Br'er Snake says, "I was in that hole, and Br'er Possum was . . ." Br'er Rabbit says, "You were where? Maybe if you show me . . ." So Br'er Snake crawls back down the hole and puts the brick on his back. Br'er Rabbit looks at him and says, "Now you stay there." And they walk away.

And Br'er Possum said, "I don't have to think about that. I ain't gonna do it."

But as Br'er Possum was talking to Br'er Snake, Br'er Snake looked pitiful. Br'er Possum, he kinda felt sorry for him. So he said, *(resigned)*

"All right, all right, you do look cold. I'm gonna put you in my pocket. But I'm gonna get you out before you get to bitin' and stabbin' and tearin' me."

So Br'er Possum picked up Br'er Snake and put him in his pocket. Went on down the road.

After a while he forgot he had Br'er Snake in his pocket. Br'er Snake commenced to coming up out of the pocket, faced Br'er Possum, and he said,

"Taaaaaaasssssssssssssssssssssss."

"I'm gonna bite you, I'm gonna bite you. *Haaaa.*

"Taaaaaaasssssssssssssssssssssssss."

And Br'er Possum said, "Why?

"I done you all of them favors, got that brick off from your back, got you out of that hole, and put you in my pocket to get you warm.

"Now you're gonna turn on me like that? *Why?*"

And Br'er Snake, he said,

"Taaaaaaassssssssssssssssssssssss.

"You know'd I was a snake when you put me in your pocket. Haa*haaaaaaaaa.*

"Taaaaaaassssssssssssssssssssssssss."

Well, my grandma didn't tell us what happened, but she did tell us that when you're walking along, minding your own business, and you spot trouble, don't *never* trouble trouble till trouble troubles you.

. . . And *that's* the end of that.

"*. . . don't NEVER trouble trouble.*"

And that's the message; all Br'er tales have simple messages, and they're pretty easy to figure out. But even when you think you know the point of the Br'er story, it doesn't really matter; the fun is getting there, hearing the details and watching the story build up.

Y ou know, Br'er Rabbit was a real good fisherman. All he had to do was take his fishin' pole down to the water, and within ten minutes he would have fifty fish. He was a *good* fisherman. That is, he was when he felt like fishing. That wasn't too often.

Br'er Rabbit had a good friend, Br'er Raccoon. He called him Br'er R'coon for short. Br'er R'coon fished, but he didn't fish for fish, he fished for *frogs*.

All Br'er R'coon had to do was take a tote sack, go down to the high grass on the river, and pick frogs.

Every day he'd fill a tote sack and carry it home.

He'd pull it up on the porch, and his wife would come out and she'd say, *(raise both arms)*

"Oh, ha*haaaaa*. *(stretch it out)* Fraaaoowwgs."

She liked frogs too.

Now, those frogs were having a *little* problem with Br'er R'coon catchin' 'em. He wasn't picky about what frogs he'd catch. Why, he was getting grandmas and grandpas and sisters and brothers and mamas and daddys and oh, it was *awful*.

So one day, a big ol' frog jumped up on a log and he said, "We got to *do* somethin' about this!"

And the other frogs said, "*Yeah*. *(pause)* What?"

"We got to stop him! He's catchin' our grandmas, he's catchin' our grandpas. We got to *stop him!*"

And the other frogs said, "Yeah, *yeah* . . . How?"

"We need us *(loud)* a lookout frog."

"Yeah," they said. "A lookout."

"We need us a lookout frog."

DIFFERENT STORY VOICES:
I completely forget all about me when I play the parts in a story. Here is a story that shows you how good gestures and a lot of different kinds of voices work to bring a child right into the story. The story has lots of details, and you know, the real pleasure in both telling and hearing stories is having fun with the voices and details. I want children to forget where the story is going, I really want them to enjoy the trip. This story is too abstract to predict, kids can't tell how Br'er Rabbit is going to pull his plan off, so they get involved with the other stuff.

"We need us a frog with big ol' ears, *(even louder)* can hear him coming from afar.

"We need a frog with a big mouth, can *warn* us.

"We need a frog with big eyes, can see'm comin'."

They said, *(pump fists)* "Yeah, yeah, yeah."

Now the only frog that fit them qualifications was the Bull Frog. They set him down on the river.

And he'd watch and he'd look and he'd listen.

And he'd watch and he'd look and he'd listen.

And when Br'er R'coon got within half a mile, you could hear that Bull Frog, *(very deep, very gruff)*

"Here he comes. Here he comes.

"Heeeeeeeeeeeeeeeeeeeere he comes."

And the little frogs would answer, *(very light, high voice)*

"Here he comes. Here he comes.

"Heeeeeeeeeeeeeeeeeeeere he comes."

And they'd all leap into the water, 'cause Br'er R'coon couldn't swim, so he couldn't catch 'em.

Seven days went by like that. Br'er R'coon kept goin' home with an empty sack.

One day he walked in, and his wife caught him, ***Barraaaaaaaaang!***

Right square in the middle of the head with a broomstick. *"Oooooooooo!"* said Br'er R'coon.

"What you do that for, woman?"

And she said, *(huffy)* "Well, how come you're comin' in this house without a frog?"

He said, "I can't catch 'em."

She said, "What do mean *you can't catch 'em?*"

He said, *(whine)* "They done got too *wild* to catch."

She said, "What do you mean too wild to catch? They's *been* wild *(angry)* and you been catchin' 'em."

"Heeeeeeeeeeeeeeeere he comes."

_____

Oh my, I do love to become these characters. I just love to act. In college I played Mama in "Raisin in the Sun," and I was Cleopatra. And I love to sing too, I'd be off somewhere singing right now if I could. But I have these nodules on my vocal cords, they give me those real deep voices. Doctors tell me, "We can take 'em off, but you'll lose those voices." Then I couldn't do the Bull Frog in this story or my ghosts. So, uh uh.

He said, "But every time I get within half a mile of that river, all you can hear is *(fast)*

"*Here he comes, here he comes, here he comes!*

"So when I get down there, they's all in the water. And *(despairing)* I can't swim."

She said, "I'm gonna starve to death and you're gonna starve to death and all your little children's gonna starve to death if you don't catch them frogs."

She said, *(raise arm)* "*Do you see this broomstick?*"

He said, "Yeah, I see it."

"Do you know what I'm gonna do with it?"

He said, "No, I don't."

She said, "I'm gonna put it on your head if you don't go and *(even angrier)* catch them frogs."

He said, "I'm gone, I'm gone, I'm gone."

"'Ooooooooo!' said Br'er R'coon."   And he took that empty tote sack and he went

down the road talking to himself. *(grumpy mumbling)*

"I *can't* catch them frogs. I tried, I done *tried*. And every time I get within half a mile I hear that

"*Here he comes, here he comes, here he comes!*"

He looked up. Comin' along from the river was his best friend Br'er Rabbit. Br'er Rabbit had been fishin' that morning, had him a big ol' line of fish, kinda draggin' along behind him.

"Well, Br'er R'coon," he said. "How you doin'?"

Br'er R'coon said, "Mmm, I ain't doing too well."

Br'er Rabbit said, "Well, I can see that, you look kinda *down* in the mouth."

And Br'er R'coon said, *(downcast)* "It ain't my mouth

"Shhhhh! Can't NOBODY hear it."

Oh yeah, they need a secret plan. Nobody could know it. You see, somebody could run right down and tell the frogs. Br'er Rabbit had to be real careful. He was a wily character, using his wits and thinking all the time. Critters could always catch Br'er Rabbit; he was used to facing bad guys and thinking his way out. All it took was knowing your enemy.

I'm down in. Do you see these knots on my head?"

"Yeah, I see 'em. How did you get 'em?"

Br'er R'coon said, "My wife give them to me with the broomstick. *(frustrated)* I can't catch any frogs. I go down to the river and every time I get within half a mile, all you can hear is

"*Here he comes, here he comes, here he comes!*

"And when I get there they all jump in the water. And you know I can't swim."

Br'er Rabbit said, "You know, Br'er R'coon, *(point)* you need a *plan* to catch them frogs."

Br'er R'coon said, "I do? What's a plan?"

Br'er Rabbit said, "Don't you worry about that, I'm the best planner that ever planned a plan. Just let me sit down here and think you up one."

So Br'er Rabbit threw his fish over the limb of a tree, sat back on his hind legs, and threw his ears up in the air. Then he took one ear *(turn, twist body)* and one hind leg, and he scratched his ear. Then he took the other hind leg, scratched the other ear, and then took the *other* hind leg, and scratched it again.

And then he said, *"AHAAA!*

"Do WHAT?"

"I got it, I got it, I got it. I got you a plan."

Br'er R'coon said, *(excited)* "Well, tell me what it is. *Teeeeeeeell* me what it is."

Br'er Rabbit said, *"Shhhhh!* Can't *nobody* hear it.

"This here is your plan. *(look both ways, whisper)* Go down to the river and when you get there, fall dead."

Br'er R'coon said, *(shocked)* "Do *WHAT?*"

"Shhhhhhh!" Br'er Rabbit said. *(look both ways again)* "Go to the river. When you get there, fall dead."

Br'er R'coon said, *(distress)* "But, I don't *wanna* die."

"*Shhhhh,*" Br'er Rabbit said. "I don't mean die, I mean *play* dead."

Br'er R'coon said, "*Ah!* What do I do after that?"

Br'er Rabbit said, "You don't do nothin'. You just lay right there 'till I tell you to move."

Br'er R'coon said, "Then we catch them frogs?"

Br'er Rabbit said, "Lay until I tell you to move. Then we'll see. Remember, don't move for nobody or nothin'. Don't move till *I* tell you to move."

Br'er R'coon said, "All right, that's a good plan. Don't know what it is, but it's a good one."

So down to the river Br'er R'coon went.

"*. . . and he commenced to die.*"

He got within half a mile when he began to hear it.

"**Here he comes. Here he comes.** *(deep Bull Frog voice)*

"**Heeeeeeeeeeeeeeeeeeeeere he comes**."

"*Here he comes. Here he comes.* *(high Little Frog voice)*

"*Heeeeeeeeeeeeeeeeeeeeere he comes.*"

Br'er R'coon didn't care, *hah*, he had him a plan. They could holler and carry on all they wanted.

He went down to the river, he lay that sack down, and he commenced to die. *(moan, groan, and tilt over)*

"*OoooommmOOOoooommaaHAAaaaaaaa.*"

It took him a while to die. **(head down, close eyes)**

The frogs never payed him one bit of attention.
In a while the sun come out and it shone right down
on Br'er R'coon and it was hot.

Br'er R'coon wanted to roll out of the sun, but
Br'er Rabbit had told him, "*Don't you move.*"

And he didn't. *Foooooooooooff.* **(fan yourself)**

After a while the flies come in and sat on his face,
crawled all across his eyes,
crawled up his nose, **(scrunch, wrinkle nose)**
crawled in and out of his ears,
and crawled across his mouth.

"OoommOOoooommaaHAaaaaa."

---

*Poor Br'er R'coon, it was real hot.
You can have fun with this, you
can make everybody see that sun
shining down and flies walking all
over him. He had to lay there, he
had to make them believe he was
dead. It was horrible, but he had
to do it, that was the secret plan.*

He sure enough wanted to move, but he didn't.

The sun went down and the flies flew off.

Down through the woods comes Br'er Rabbit.
He walked over to Br'er R'coon, looked out and saw
the frogs all swimming around, havin' a good time.

Br'er Rabbit commenced to crying.

"*Whooo**oo**Whooo**o**Whoo**Whoo**o**Whooooo.*"

Finally the frogs got curious and crawled up
on the bank. The Bull Frog stood by Br'er R'coon,

and hollered up at Br'er Rabbit.

"What's the matter witcha? (deep Bull Frog voice)**

"What's the matter witcha?

"Whaaaaaaaaat's the matter witcha?"

"What's the matter witcha? (high Little Frog voice)*

"What's the matter witcha?

"Whaaaaaaaaaat's the matter witcha?"

Br'er Rabbit said, "This's my friend Br'er R'coon. He's done fell dead here. He's dead, *he's dead.*"

And the Bull frog said,

"That's good. That's good. (deep Bull Frog voice)**

"Thaaat's goooooooooooood."

"That's good. That's good. (high Little Frog voice)*

"Thaaat's goooooooooooood."

Br'er Rabbit said, *(sob)* "I promised if he should die before me, I'd bury him in the place he loved best.

"...got out their little frog shovels."

And he loved this river. I'm gonna dig him a grave right on this bank and bury him right here."

And the Bull frog said,

"***Let us dig it. Let us dig it.*** *(deep Bull Frog voice)*

"***Let uuuuuuuuuuuuuuuus dig it.***"

"*Let us dig it. Let us dig it.* *(high Little Frog voice)*

"*Let uuuuuuuuuuuuuuuuus dig it.*"

Br'er Rabbit said, "Well, that's mighty fine of you. Seein' I'm so torn up with grief and all, I'm gonna let you dig the grave. I'll tell you how deep to dig it."

The frogs gathered around Br'er R'coon, got out their little frog shovels, and commenced to diggin'.

They was diggin' dirt from under Br'er R'coon, they was diggin' dirt *(arms up both ways)* every which way, little frogs, big frogs, old frogs. That dirt was flyin'.

Old Br'er R'coon was kinda layin' there waitin'.

". . . and commenced to diggin'."

Oh, children love things like this; they send me pictures of frog shovels you just wouldn't believe. My goodness, they're so cute; some of them are green, some of them have tiny spots, and some even have pretty little curlicues. Why kids think frog shovels have curlicues on them, I don't know.

Soon the grave was ten feet deep. The Bull Frog leaped up on Br'er R'coon's belly and hollered,

"*Izzzz it deep enough? Izzzz it deep enough?*"
"*Izzzzzzzzz it deep enough?*"
"*Izzzz it deep enough? Izzzz it deep enough?*"
"*Izzzzzzzzz it deep enough?*"

Br'er Rabbit said, "Well, can you all jump out?"
The Bull Frog looked around to see.

"*Yes, we can. Yes, we can. Yeeeeeeees, we can.*"
"*Yes, we can. Yes, we can. Yeeeeeeees, we can.*"

"Well, it ain't deep enough. Dig it deeper."

The Bull Frog and the other frogs commenced to diggin' again. That dirt was really comin' up, but

"Izzzzzzzzzz it deep enough?"

Ah yes, the rhythm of all the frog voices, that's what people always remember. The deep Bull Frog voice. Children join in and I kinda like that, it helps me and lets me rest sometimes. In the afternoon it's nice to rest and I let them say it as long as they want. And they try to make that voice too. Hah!

they were gettin' tired. Some could barely lift dirt up and some were just layin' on ol' Br'er R'coon.

Ol' Br'er R'coon was just layin' there waitin'.

Oh, those frogs were tired. Some had fallen over Br'er R'coon's belly, *(slump over)* some laid on his face, they just couldn't dig any longer. The Bull Frog climbed on Br'er R'coon's chest and hollered,

"*Izzz it deep enough? Izzz it deep enough?* (slower)
"*Izzzzzzzzz it deep enough?*"

161   Br'er Rabbit Outsmarts the Frogs

Br'er Rabbit said, "Well, can you all jump out?"
The Bull Frog looked up to see.
"***Belieeeve we can. Belieeeve we can.*** *(exhausted)*
"***Belieeeeeeeeeeeeeeeve we can.***"
"*Belieeeve we can. Belieeeve we can.* *(exhausted)*
"*Belieeeeeeeeeeeeeve we can.*"
Br'er Rabbit said, *(look way down, cup mouth)* "Well,
it ain't deep enough yet. You gotta dig it deeper."
Soon they just couldn't go any further. The grave
was 12 feet deep and they couldn't dig another inch.
Frogs were all laid out in the bottom of the grave,
laid all over Br'er R'coon. The Bull Frog crawled up
on Br'er R'coon's chin and hollered out of the grave,
"***Izzz it deep enough? Izzz it deep enough?*** *(spent)*
"***Izzzzzzzzzzz it deep enough?***"
"*Izzz it deep enough? Izzz it deep enough?* *(spent)*
"*Izzzzzzzzzz it deep enough?*"
Br'er Rabbit said, "Well, can you all jump out?"
The Bull Frog looked around and he said,
"***Nooo, we can't. Nooo, we can't.*** *(worn out, look up)*
"***Noooooooooooooo, we can't.***"
"*Nooo, we can't. Nooo, we can't.* *(very droopy, look up)*
"*Noooooooooooooo, we can't.*"
Br'er Rabbit said, "***GET UP, BR'ER R'COON,
AND GRAB YOUR GROCERIES! THEY'S TOO
TIRED TO JUMP OUT OF THAT HOLE.***"
And Br'er R'coon leaped up, grabbed that sack,
filled it full of frogs, and took 'em home.
His wife was very happy; they had enough frogs
to do 'em this year and next year to boot. *Hah!*

. . . And *that's* the end of that.

Family Tales

FAMILY TALES

I got a line of stories about my family that I want to tell so bad it makes my nose itch. But I really think everybody does, everybody has family memories which become stories, which become a kind of family history. Like the pictures in their photograph album, these stories are important to a family. They're important to remember, they need to be told and told again 'cause they keep the people you loved alive, just like the pictures do.

When I look at my family pictures I can't help but remember all those good times. Like the times my granddaddy told me the stories I still tell today. But he was sick, you know, he was sick all the time. I remember how I felt when he died. I didn't understand what death was, they just told me he went to heaven. Mmm, I didn't like heaven so much 'cause it took my granddaddy. One day I was sitting on the

"Don't you sing about heaven."

porch with my aunt Sally. It was Saturday, it had to be Saturday because that's when Aunt Sally would comb her beautiful long hair. Then she'd wet it all and grease it and wrap it up with pieces of string. On Sunday morning, when she'd shake it loose, it would all be curly and wavy, but she'd still pack it back in that bun to go to church.

But while she wrapped her hair with those strings, she would sing, "*All God's children got shoes . . . When I get to heaven, gonna put on m'shoes . . . Gonna shout all over God's heaven . . .*" And I looked up at Aunt Sally and I said, "Don't you sing about heaven." She looked down at me and she said, "Lord, child, why are you so mad about heaven?" I said, "Aunt Sally, heaven took Granddaddy and it didn't give him back." And she reached for me. I was getting to be a big girl then, but she pulled me up on her lap and she said, "You know, your granddaddy was mighty sick. He couldn't eat, he couldn't walk, he couldn't sleep, and he was all thin." She said, "He went to heaven, and heaven is the place that cures everything. Right at this minute your granddaddy is soppin' corn bread in buttermilk. In about two hours he's gonna have him some cathead biscuits with sweet butter and molasses. He can eat anything he wants and it won't hurt him. And I bet you anything he's walking all over heaven 'cause he left his walking cane right here. He has no need for it. He's fat and he's not feeling one single pain." Well, I kind of thought about that. I thought, "Well now, heaven might not be so bad after all."

Oh, that was a good time for me to remember, and Aunt Sally had given it to me. There was magic in stories about my family, and I pass that magic along. If you've got a family album, get it out. Look through it. Find the people and the days that were magic for you,

"... if you really feel the magic ..."

find the stories that your family needs to remember. You can dress them up a bit and mix them around if you want, but hold on to what's important. Keep the basic things, don't forget the universal truths like love, hate, and fear. Then practice your story alone. If it sounds good to your ear, then you're the best judge. If your listener is young, if you have a three-year-old child, think like that child, you know what he or she likes. But tell them the story the way you want to, just go ahead, tell them the story. If they don't like it, they'll fall asleep or crawl out the front door, but go ahead and tell it. Just remember, if you really feel the magic in the stories you tell about your family, if you really feel it, others will feel that magic too. That's what I do.

THE BABY SALE

It had been a long day at the library. And it was even longer because it was inventory. During the day *thousands* of books had passed through my hands. It was 10 o'clock at night. All I wanted to do was close my eyes and go to sleep.

As I walked in the house, the baby-sitter said, "She's not asleep. Good night."

"Oh no," I thought. That was my daughter Lori. She always falls asleep about nine o'clock; why was she awake *tonight?* I went into the bedroom.

She said, *(perky and smiling)* "Hi, Mama."

"We're up for the rest of the night," I thought.

"Hello, what are you doing awake?" I said.

She said, *(sweetly)* "I was waiting on you."

"Wonderful. Why were you waiting on me?"

"I wanna hear a story," she said.

"Well, all right, I'll read a story," I said.

"No, I wanna hear a story from your *mouth.*" Well, that meant she wanted me to *tell* her a story, not read a story from a book.

"Wonderful. What story do you want to hear?" She thought about it awhile, and then she said,

"I wanna hear where I come from."

I thought, "Oh no, not the birds and bees tonight." Then I said, "Lori, would you like to hear the truth, or would you like to hear a story?"

She said, "I'd like to hear a story."

"Oh, good," I thought. Well, I sat there thinking for a long time, and then I began.

"'I wanna hear a story,' she said."

CREATING FAMILY STORIES:
A good family story has pieces of truth in it. It has a familiar thing or a familiar place, or something very special about the family that everybody knows. Around those little truths, you create a story you make up. When my daughter Lori asked where she came from, she didn't want the real facts, she wanted a story. But right at the end I added a bit of truth to it anyway, something special about Lori that only the family knew.

"Not the birds and the bees . . ."

You have to walk around certain things, you know, like the birds and the bees. Do you give them too much, or not enough, or just the right amount? I was lucky when Lori wanted a story; I just didn't feel like figuring all of that out. The story lasted about 30 minutes when I told it for the first time, 'cause Lori asked a million questions. "Well, where was it? What side of Salisbury was it on? What was the nurse's name?" Then the story got longer each time I told it because I had to add my answers to all her questions.

Once upon a time, your dad and I decided we were just a little lonesome. If we had a little baby, we thought, it might keep us company, keep us from being so alone. He said, "Where do you think we ought to get one?"

"Well, today is Sunday. Why don't we look in the newspaper; there might be some sales."

So I opened up the great big Sunday paper, and I turned *(swing arms)* from page to page.

And there it was, *(eyes wide)* *a whole-page spread.* *BABY SALE!* At the Rowan County Hospital Nursery Store. *EVERYTHING MUST GO!*

"That's where I'll go and buy myself a baby," I thought. I tore the page out and folded it up, and placed it in my purse. The next morning, just as the Nursery Store opened, I walked in.

"Good morning," I said to the clerk.

"Good morning. May I help you?"

"Yes," I said. *(cheery)* "I'm looking for a baby."

"Oh," she said. "How sweet. We've got lots of them. Just take your choice."

"Well, I'd like one that sort of fits me."

"All right. Let me show you some," she said.

Well, it seemed that all the babies were kept in little shoe boxes on the shelves. She brought a nice little shoe box over to me, placed it on the counter, and opened the top. I looked inside and I saw a cute little baby. It had great big black eyes and beautiful black hair. Oooh, but its complexion?

I didn't recognize it. It was kind of *different.*

"I think this is an *Asian* baby," I said.

"Mmm, I don't think I can use *this* one."

"...a whole-page spread."

I thought of the "Baby Sale" story because Lori and I were doing a lot of shopping together at the time. She was real big on looking in boxes. When I'd look around in a store and couldn't see her, she was always under a counter looking in a box. "Mama, here's something they don't have up there," she would say. Lori was a real shopper, and I knew this was the kind of story she'd like.

"That's all right," she said. "I have others."
She put that box back and brought me another.

"How is this?" she said.

"*Ooooo, look*, that's an *Indian* baby," I said.

"Yes," she said. "But isn't it cute?"

"Oh, they're *all* so cute, I'd like to take them *all* home, but I'm not sure whether they would fit me."

"Don't worry, we'll find you one," she said.

Oooh, *(long sigh)* some of them were so beautiful. In fact, they were *all* beautiful. Some were black, some were white, some were Japanese. Oh my, so many babies, I just couldn't choose. I couldn't find one that fit me just right.

"Do you have any more?" I asked.

"No, all of our stock is on the shelves," she said.

"Oh my, so many babies . . ."

"You don't have any in the back?" I asked.

"No, everything's out."

"Well, could you give me a rain check then?"

"Oh no, I'm very sorry," she said. "We don't give rain checks for Baby Sales."

I said, *(very disappointed)* "Oh."

"Well," I said, "if you don't have any more babies, I guess I'll come back later."

"Just a minute," she said. "Just before I opened, I put one baby in the back. The box was very wet, but I can change it."

"No, that's all right, let me see it," I said.

"Well, if you don't mind a wet box . . ."

So she brought out the little wet box. And it was indeed wet. She opened the top. *(lift hand, look down)*

"*Oooooooh*," I said. "*Look at that baby.*"
It was brown all over, it had black curly hair, and it had great big black eyes.

I turned it over.

Oh! On its little backside it had a tiny little mole, shaped just like a star. *(laugh)*

Had one on its foot too. *(longer laugh)*

"Oh, I *like* this one," I said, "it looks *just* like me."

"Well, I can change the box," she said. "The only thing wrong is the box. It's so *wet*."

"It's fine," I said. "I'll take it, box and all."

So I took it home, and you know what?

That box was *never* dry, it was always wet.

My daughter looked up at me.

She said, *(sweetly)* "That was me, wasn't it?"

And I said, "Yes . . . it was."

. . . And *that's* the end of that.

"*. . . it had a tiny little mole . . .*"

Actually, Lori has two moles. She could see the mole on her foot, but she couldn't see the one on her bottom. When she was little, I always talked about it when I washed her, and told her where it was. My story said that a child with a mole like that was special. I was saying, "I like this one baby because she has something that makes her different." Even the wet box was special. It belonged in the story because that's what all babies do. Lori has a baby of her own now, and he wets his own box. And everywhere else.

"*That was me, wasn't it?*"

Good family stories come from anywhere, and they grow and grow as you retell them. Just be sure that you remember them; that's the most important thing. Parents often tell a story and then they totally forget it. "Tell me the story you told last night," your child says, and you can't remember it. If you know you've told a good story, make some notes. Right away. Even today, more than 20 years after I first told this Baby Sale story, I must always remember every detail. If I don't, Lori says, "Mama, you forgot about the wet box." Well, I can't forget about the wet box, the wet box is very important.

Now, when I was four years old, the person that stood out in my life, the one I liked best of all, was my aunt Sally. I *loved* Aunt Sally. Aunt Sally was a fat woman. I loved Aunt Sally 'cause she was a golden brown all over. Her color was smooth, like hot chocolate with cream in it. And her skin was *soft*, it always had a little shine to it, as I remember.

Her hair was long and black and real coarse. It was thick and heavy hair. When she made a braid it wasn't thin, it was *thick*. So she kept it in a bun on the back of her head all the time.

But when she'd untie it, it would say, *"Poooof!"* and hair (both hands way up and out) was all over the place.

Well, I liked Aunt Sally because when she walked she had a little jiggle. I used to walk behind her and watch that and think about it.

"Wouldn't it be nice if I could jiggle like that?"

And so I used to say that to my grandmother.

"I want to jiggle like Aunt Sally," I said.

Now, to a woman like my grandmother, who was like my mother, 98 pounds, that was disgraceful.

"You know, Sally's got too much behind.

"And Sally's got too much in front too."

She always wore low-cut dresses. And so a lot of her popped out, you know, and I liked that too. I could just see myself with all of that jiggling up in front of me and behind me too.

And so I'd say, "I want to look like Aunt Sally."

"I want to jiggle like Aunt Sally."

USING THE FAMILY MEMORIES:
Yes, tiny bits of truth and familiar things make a family story real. If the grandpa in your story has a walking cane, you can make that cane magic. If your child has a special feature, like crossed toes, use them in a story and add more things around them. Maybe you tell a story about a room full of a million cats. How in the world could you pick one special cat in that room? "Look, there's a cat with crossed toes!" you'd say. You know you couldn't find more than one like that, you know it's a special cat. Now the child has been given a story, a family story that will always be remembered.

My grandmother would look down at me.

"You'd better watch out what you ask God for," she said. "He may give it to you."

Well now, I was blessed with Aunt Sally's jiggle. And I had to deal with it because I asked for it. You know, my grandmother said, if I asked for it . . .

Aunt Sally smelled *goood*. I didn't know what it was, but when I'd go near her she smelled just like a pound cake. Now, you have not smelled *anything* until you have smelled the first odor of a pound cake baking in the oven. That's how Aunt Sally smelled.

And it makes your mouth water.

I don't care how old or how young you are, that first smell of that pound cake, if it's made right, it's gonna make you salivate.

Aunt Sally smelled like that all the time.

And I didn't know why.

Grandma said she used vanilla flavoring for perfume. To a four-year-old, what could that mean?

Well, one day Grandma was making a cake in a great big old bowl. She didn't need a mixer, she could whip that batter *(twirl hand)* with her *hand*. I tried to do that once, and I didn't do anything but knock my finger. It got all swollen up.

But Grandma could take her hand, and with these fingers *(hold up fingers)* she could whip that batter. The cake would be smooth and soft, no air bubbles.

Well, she was whipping that cake, you know, with these little bottles on the table. Course, I talked all the time, and so I asked her what *that* was,

"Aunt Sally smelled GOOOD."

And her hair! Oh, her hair was so beautiful. I used to dream about having hair like that. But mine wouldn't puff up like Aunt Sally's did. I remember in the sixties, when Afros were in, I got my hair like hers one time, but it was too heavy to stay puffed up and it fell right down. Boy, that Aunt Sally, she had her some pretty hair.

and what *that* was and *that* was, and she told me
coconut flavoring, banana flavoring, walnut flavoring,
and then she said, *"That's* vanilla flavoring."

Aaahaaaaah . . .

And so, when she had her back turned, I takes
the vanilla flavoring and go outside.

Then I pour that vanilla all over me!

Well, the gnats stuck to me, (slap hands around face)
and the flies were after me,

and the bees caught sight of the flies after me
and they figured it was something good going on,
and they come in too!

Well, finally, when Grandma caught me, I mean
I was doing *90 miles an hour* around the house.

"Girl! *You going to get sunstroke!"* she said.

Well, then she caught me and took a whiff of me.

"Well, the gnats stuck to me . . ."

I tell ya, vanilla flavoring and that first whiff of pound cake in the oven brings Aunt Sally right back to me. I liked her a lot. She was a large woman and there was a gold glimmer on her front teeth when she smiled. I can see that woman when I tell her stories.

By that time, the vanilla flavoring had changed
to something else, you know, with the body heat and
the sweat and everything.

She said, "My God, *what have you been into?*"

And I tried to explain to her what happened.

And she said, "Well now, you dumb old thing,
Aunt Sally just uses a little bit behind the ears.
She don't draw gnats and flies and bees like this."

Noooo, she didn't. *(lean forward)*

She drew *men*.

Aunt Sally had five husbands. She was married
five times. I didn't know but one husband,
and that was the one she had when I was a little girl.

John Wilson was his name.

Grandpa said that John Wilson had to be
the ignorantest man God ever blew breath into.

And Grandma hated him.

But she didn't let on, you know.

At first I didn't know that this man had a name,
but I would hear people whisper, you know. When
you're little you can get around, hear lots of things.
I would hear them say, "Here comes Miss Sally
and that fifth husband of hers."

Or "Here comes Miss Sally's fifth husband."

So I heard the word "fifth" all the time.

So I called him Uncle Fifth.

He didn't know why. I mean, he didn't think.
I used to get on his lap and say, *"Hey, Uncle Fifth."*

And he'd say to Pa, "Jim, I just don't know why
this gal calls me Uncle Fifth."

And Pa would look over at Grandma and say,
"See what I mean?"

"Aunt Sally had five husbands."

She was one powerful character,
Aunt Sally was, she was a reader
and a seer. She predicted the
future, and she'd tell you what
death was and all sorts of things
like that. She was also a clown.
As my grandfather said, "She's
up to fool and folly all the time."
She kept my grandma scared of
things, kept her goin' all the time.
She would come to the edge of
her porch and she'd holler down,
"Watch out now, there's a convict
loose and he's headed this way!"
Grandma would race around the
house locking all the doors and
windows. That was Aunt Sally,
you never knew what came next.

I *loved* Aunt Sally and Uncle Fifth.

Uncle Fifth was kind of stupid, you know, but I liked him anyway. We'd go to church and Aunt Sally would walk in, with me behind her trying to walk just like her, and she'd pull into the pew. Uncle Fifth would sit on the end, she'd sit beside him, and I'd sit beside her and Grandma. Pa always sat up front.

Somebody would come over and say, "*Hello*, Miss Sally.

"My, that's a *fine* brooch you've got on."

And Aunt Sally would know what they were looking at. She always wore long sleeves 'cause she had big arms. She'd take that fan out of her sleeve, open it up, and say, "Well, *thank you*, Mr. Jones.

"*For recognizing* (fan yourself) *my brooch.*"

And my grandmother would say, "Do Jesus!"

"Well, THANK YOU, Mr. Jones."

She sure liked to be playful. But then she'd sit down in church and play the organ and she'd be all business. She'd start a song and everybody would just lay out shouting and carrying on. She had a lot of talents and she was smart, funny, and colorful. To be like Aunt Sally, to have that kind of grand manner, that'd be nice.

Then she'd tell Pa at home, "That sister of yours is an out-and-out *huzzzy*." Now, what could a four-year-old know about being a huzzzy? If they meant Aunt Sally, then *I* wanted to be a huzzzy.

I'd practice, *(softly)* "Huzzzy! Huzzzy! Huzzzy!"

I could see myself looking like Aunt Sally and doing what huzzzies do, whatever that was. One day a lady asked me what I wanted to be when I grew up.

"I want to be a huzzzy like my aunt Sally."

You don't *hear* people faint, but you could hear my grandmother, "*Aahhh!*" Bam! She hit the floor.

My aunt Sally about died laughing.

Well, Grandma washed my mouth out with soap. Didn't stop me, though.

"One day a lady asked me..."
"I want to be a huzzzy..."

... And *that's* the end of that.

DEXTER THE DOG

Years later, all of my uncles got together and started talking about Sally's different husbands. And they talked about Milo. Milo was husband number two, and he was real light-skinned. This was way before my time, 'cause my uncles were teenagers, or even younger.

They said Milo had real good hair and blue eyes. They said they thought he was white for a while, but he was just light, you know, and he looked good.

He was a big handsome fellow.

And he loved Aunt Sally.

Milo had been a chauffeur in New York.

Back in the thirties, when the family he worked for had sorta died out, they left him the car.

It was a big old car, a Hudson.

But they said, "We don't want it anymore," and they gave it to him. That car is what he brought to the marriage, 'cause Aunt Sally had all this slave land that her daddy had left her.

It was a real nice car. Aunt Sally didn't want him to drive it, so they kept the car covered all week until Saturday. Then she would dress up and they would go to town. He'd make her sit in the back, like the women he used to drive in New York.

Well, he wanted Aunt Sally to have a poodle too.

But they couldn't afford a poodle.

Aunt Sally didn't have nothing but an old hound, a sooner hound named Dexter.

You know, sooner one kinda dog as the other.

Dexter was a big ol' yellow dog.

Had hair *(circle arms)* all over him.

So Milo took a straight razor to Dexter and he just shaved him naked, all except for these four great big old puff balls around the bottom of his feet.

And Dexter had great big feet.

Big old clumsy dog, he was, with a long tail.

So Milo shaved all of Dexter's tail too, except for a great big ball of thick fur between the middle of his tail and the end of it.

You know, so he would look like a poodle.

But they couldn't do anything with the great big bearded mane that Dexter had, so they just left it.

Old Dexter was just layin' on the porch one day, Uncle James said, and when he laid down, his tail kind of stretched out across the front of him. When he got up his tail got up too and it bounced around.

Scared poor old Dexter somethin' awful.

He took off into the woods and it took four days to catch him. His tail just scared him to death.

Every time he'd turn around it was still after him.

So Aunt Sally would have to sit in the car and hold Dexter 'cause now he was scared of everything. He had never ridden in anything but a wagon before, and this automobile was scaring him to death too.

Well, then there was my uncle Len.

Uncle Len left home in 1949, never came back for anything . . . he just left. He was a bad boy.

He was a big old liar.

Pa and Grandma tried everythin', but he still lied.

"He was a big old liar."

Sometimes there are things you want to tell a child, things you care about like lying. Tales about people in your family can help you. Every family has Uncle Len, and when you feel a child is not telling the truth, you might say, "Let me tell you a story about my uncle Len." Then you talk about a funny dog and you laugh about it, but you are really talking about honesty and character. You can show somebody in a story who always lied and cheated and was always in trouble because of it.

One day, Uncle James said, when Uncle Len was fifteen years old, everybody came home from school by two o'clock, except Uncle Len.

They waited and waited till it was ten o'clock.

Pa was sitting out on the porch in the cold when Uncle Len come over the hill. When he got to the porch he was cryin', tears just *shootin'* outta his eyes.

Pa said, "Leonard, *(very stern) where have you been?*"

Leonard was crying so hard, he couldn't tell him.

Pa said, "Leonard, just you calm down now. I'm your papa, tell me what's wrong."

He said, "Papa, when I got ahalfway to school this morning, this lion jumped out of the woods. He chased me, and he wouldn't let me go to school."

Pa said, "Leonard, *(distressed)* you're *hurtin' me*.

"We done everything under God's sun to keep

"...tears just SHOOTIN' outta..."

Details you create and add to the story make it more interesting. Tears just shootin' out his eyes? Children can see that. Children know the feeling, the hard work it takes to make a lie believable. Everybody knew what Dexter looked like, but Grandpa, he was still supposed to believe that a lion was running around loose!

you from lying," he said. "But *you lie to lie!*"

Pa said, "I can't take that. Now, you know good and well there ain't no lions around here."

He said, "Yes there is, Papa."

Pa said, "Son, you know they done messed up that old dog, Sally's sooner hound, made it look like a lion. You know good and well that ain't no lion."

"Well, at first I didn't know it was Dexter," Leonard said. "But he chased me, and I went too far to get back to school in time."

Pa said, "*That's it!* I can't beat you no more, I'm scared I may kill you. *(point stiffly) Get in that closet!*

"If you stay there for ten years, I ain't gonna care. We'll feed you through the door. Don't come out of there until you ask God to forgive you for lying.

"And you promise God you won't lie no more. Then you wait until God says you can come out."

Leonard didn't say anything against that.

He was obedient. He went in the closet.

Grandma said, "*Ooooh Lord!*" and she fainted.

She could just see her son dying in that closet with Pa still sitting there, shaking his walking cane.

Fifteen minutes later, Uncle Len walked out.

Pa said, "Leonard, what are you doin' out here?"

Uncle Len said, "Well, God told me to come out."

Pa said, "Leonard, God told you to come out?"

Leonard said, "God told me it was all right."

Pa said, "Leonard, what did God tell you?"

Leonard said, "God said it's all right. First time he saw Dexter, he thought he was a lion too."

. . . And *that's* the end of that.

"GET IN THAT CLOSET!"

Poor Uncle Len, nothing really worked out for him. He went to Chicago, worked in Al Capone's old garage, and he never really did come back home. But, this story about Dexter is funny and it sort of saves Uncle Len in the end without losing its point.

Scary Tales

SCARY TALES

I guess I like scary tales so much because my granddaddy liked scary tales. He'd have to tell one if it killed him. He was sick a lot, but if visitors came, he'd prop himself up in an armchair and put a quilt on his lap. So nobody could see his nightshirt. Then he'd put his derby hat on, he loved that derby, and somebody would say, "Mr. Jim, tell us about that time when the fire dog followed you down though the wheat field." And my grandma would say, "Hold it, let me leave the room, lightning's going to strike." She always said Granddaddy was the biggest liar God ever blew breath into. So she'd leave, but not me. I'd get closer to Pa 'cause I wanted to watch the people listening to him.

There used to be an old man who came to our house named Hall. I would hear people say, "Mr. Hall wears a rug." I didn't know what a rug was. I'd lay down on the floor and Grandma would say, "What are you doing?" "I'm trying to find Mr. Hall's rug." And Grandma would say, "Get up, *get up!* That ain't nice." Well, one day Mr. Hall was there and Grandpa started into one of his scary stories. There was a piece of wood burning in the fireplace, sort of sticking out, and Pa spotted it. I watched him put his tobacco way back in his mouth so he could get a good long shot. At just the right moment in the story, he threw his head forward and that tobacco came out and hit that wood just right; it fell off on the floor and the fire sparked up. Somebody threw a baby on the floor, men ran out, and Mr. Hall ran out too. When he passed us, Mr. Hall's scalp was as naked as the palm of my hand. *Jesus have mercy!* Granddaddy scared the hair right off Mr. Hall's head! Well, I went over to his chair, and there in Mr. Hall's hat was his scalp! I picked it up. "Grandma! Is this Mr. Hall's rug?" Grandma said, "Put that thing down and go wash your hands." Oh, I loved those days when Grandpa told his scary stories.

So when I started telling stories in school, that's what I chose, scary tales. I've got storytelling friends who'd rather be killed than go to junior high. But not me, I love junior high. That's sixth, seventh, and eighth grade, and those kids can't believe they're going to have to sit there and listen to me tell a story. So I do just what Grandpa said, "If you want to get the attention of a mule who's too stubborn to listen, you take the branch off a tree and come right down across the top of his head." What is my branch? A good scary story. When I tell those kids, "I'm going to scare you," when I start to give them a little bit of fear, well, they're ready to listen.

A lot of people have told me I really shouldn't tell children scary things. Well, children can frighten themselves without your help. When they're alone in bed they hear things and they see things. So I just help them along. "It's *daaaaaaark*," I say. And there's a strange voice, "Where's Myy Haaairy Toe . . ." That's all they need. They remember the dark and they're scared again and that's good.

Children need to be frightened. We all do. It's an emotion that was given to all of us and it should be exercised. When you don't exercise it, you lose your sense of fear. That's why my granddaddy told me scary stories. He wanted me to know that only fools rush in where angels fear to tread. You should be a little hesitant sometimes, his stories were saying, you should think twice before you go into the

"Is this Mr. Hall's rug?"

woods, there just might be a hairy man and you need to be cautious.

My grandfather scared me to death. Grandma would say, "Get up on your granddaddy's lap and kiss him good night." I'd throw my arms around him and say, "I'm going to bed." And he'd say, "It's dark up there." And I'd say, "I know." "You know what's in the dark?" "Nooooo." "Monsters," he'd say. "What do monsters do?" "They'll drag you off the bed and put you in the keyhole," he'd say. Well, I yelled and screamed going up the stairs. My grandmother would say to me on the way up, "*Would you stop crying? There's not a keyhole big enough to put you in.*" So I remained fat for the rest of my life. That's why no monsters have ever bothered me.

ELVIRA AND HENRY

Now, Elvira and Henry lived *way* out in the country. And Elvira got a letter from her sister saying she was feeling bad, and she needed them to come over and help her with her farm. She had been in bed for three weeks and it didn't look like she would be able to get out and work. The cows needed milking.

Elvira said, "Henry, let's go and help my sister."

And Henry said, *(gruff and deep)* "Well . . . all right."

Elvira said, *(gently)* "Can we go tomorrow?"

Elvira

"Oh, all right, Henry . . ."

A FAVORITE STORY GROWS:
This is the first scary story that I wrote, and it shows how a story can grow larger and larger as you retell it. I started to write it in the fifth grade and I got an A for it. Then every year I added more to it and handed it in until James, the class tattletale, told on me.

Henry said, "Well, let's get going before dark."

"Oh, all right, Henry," Elvira said, "you hook up Ned and I'll go pack the bag."

And Henry said, *(annoyed)* "Elvira, if you want to go, you pack up that bag and you fix up Ned too."

She said, *(gently)* "Oh, all right."

So Elvira packed the bag and hooked Ned up to the wagon and they took off.

Two weeks they spent with Elvira's sister, until

finally she was up and well, and she said,

"Elvira, I thank you so much for you and Henry coming over. I feel real good. I'm going to be able to take care of everything myself now."

"Oh," Elvira said. "You're going to be all right?"

"Oh yes," her sister said.

So Elvira went to Henry. "Henry, my sister says she's all right. So we can go home in the morning."

Henry said, *(really annoyed)* "We leaving *tonight*."

"Oh," Elvira said, "Henry, clouds are coming up out there. And this here's wintertime, you know. I don't think we ought to be traveling on that road. It's going to get *dark* before we get home."

He said, *(very surly)* "We leaving *tonight*."

"But, *(whining)* Henry . . ."

"You go *(point, very gruff)* and hook up Ned."

"Oh, *(sweet again)* all right."

So she hooked up the wagon and they took off.

And sure enough, it started to snow. The snow turned to sleet, and the sleet turned to cold rain, and the rain turned to icicles on Elvira's nose.

Elvira began to complain to Henry.

"Henry, *(moaning)* my *nose* is cold. My ears are cold and my toes are cold. This wagon's getting hard. I can't ride on it much longer."

And Henry said, "*Sic sic*, get on up there, Ned. Quiet your mouth, Elvira. *Sic sic*, get on there."

"Oh, Henry, don't do me this, I'm *cold!*" she said. "There ain't no way in the world we can get home. See how the ice is standing up on that mule's back? We're going to *freeeze* to death, and that old mule is going to die right where he's standing.

I was really so lazy. At first it was just Mr. Henry and Ned on a scary road on Halloween night. In the sixth grade I added Elvira and got an A plus. Then I added even more to the story in the seventh grade, and my teacher said, "This girl has written a wonderful story. I've got a good mind to flunk the rest of you." Ooooops! Up goes James' hand. He said, "I know why it's such a good story, she's been writing on it for forty years." So I couldn't use it anymore.

Not only do stories grow as you retell them, parts of them come from all sorts of places. Like the names in this story, they came from Grandpa. All his characters were named Elvira or Henry, and they would always be digging for haunted treasure. If they said a single word, that treasure would disappear. After digging for sixty hours, you know, they'd see the top of it and Henry, he would say, "My goodness," or Elvira would scream 'cause she saw a snake, "Aaaah!" and the ground would swallow it up again. Always.

"Oh, Henry, *(whimper)* please let's stop," Elvira said.

"*Get up there Ned.* You be *quiet*, Elvira."

"Oh, Henry. I'm telling you, I'm cold!"

Just as the wagon rounded a curve in the road, there up on a hill stood a great big old house.

And every light was on in the house.

Elvira said, *(excited)* "*Henry! Look!* There's a house! Let's stop there! *Let's stop there.*"

"Elvira, do you know who lives there?"

"No, Henry, I don't know."

"Well, I don't either. And I *ain't* stopping."

"Oh, *Henry!* My nose is cold and my ears . . ."

"Oh, *all right!*"

"*You be QUIET, Elvira.*"
"*Henry! Look! There's a house!*"

Oh Lord, this story has grown for many years, and Elvira and Henry have become really familiar to children. They're married, Henry is lazy, and they bicker a lot, and all that seems typical in families. Children like to hear about happy married couples too, but they find them, you know, a little different.

And Henry pulled the mule to a screeching halt.

"*Whoa there, mule!*" he said.

"Now listen, Elvira, go in there and find out if we can sleep in the barn or in front of the fireplace. And find out where to put this old mule tonight."

"But, Henry, I don't know them folks. You do it."

"Do you want to stay here?"

"Yes," she said.

"Well, *you* do it then," he said.

And Elvira said, "Well then, you find somewhere to put that old mule and then you come on in."

Henry said, *(grudging)* "All right."

And Elvira leaped down from the wagon.

Henry said, "Get up there, Ned," and pulled away.

Elvira went up to the door.

It was a big old door; she had never seen a door so big. She raised her hand and she knocked.

Boom . . . Boom . . . Boommm.

Somewhere in the back of the house she heard, "*Come innnnnnnnn.*"

Elvira said, "Somebody's in there." She turned the huge doorknob and pushed the door open.

EEEEEEEEEEeeeerrrrrrrrkkkkkk.

Oh! That door hadn't been open in a long time.

Elvira stepped inside. There was nobody there

to greet her. She said, *"Hellooo!* Is anybody home?

"I'm coming in. *(loud)* Is it all right?"

But *(quietly)* nobody said a word.

So she said again, "Hello! *Hello!* Hello?"

She walked down the long hallway looking from one room to the other. There was nobody there.

But the house was warm and light and bright, and all of a sudden, *(sniff)* she smelled food cooking. She looked to her right, and there was a dining room with a table fit for a king. There was a turkey and there was a ham. And biscuits and cakes and pies, and *(wide smile)* a big pot of steaming hot coffee.

"Oh!" Elvira said. *(loud)* "I'm tasting your supper."

But *(quietly)* nobody said a word.

So she lifted the cup and pot and poured herself a cup of coffee. *(sniff, sniff)* Oh, it smelled so *good.*

"So she lifted the cup and pot ..."

Stretch the story, see the story surroundings in your mind, take time with the details, invent new stuff as you go along. You are adding the elements you need to build that story triangle as high as you can. The house has every sign of comfort, coffee and all. That's the Haint's trick to get you inside because probably, when all was said and done, this house was an old, awful-looking place.

She quickly *(raise hand)* lifted the cup to her lips.

As she placed her lips on the brim of the cup, she saw a door on the other side of the room. She stopped, put the cup back in the saucer, and took it with her as she went to the door. Just before she pushed the door open, she remembered the noise the other door made, so she pushed this one quickly.

EEEeeerrrrrrrrrkkk. *(shorter squeak)*

It hadn't been opened lately either.

She looked around the room. There on the wall were shelves and shelves and shelves of books. In the back of the room there was a huge fireplace, with a nice hot blazing fire. In front of the fireplace were two great big comfortable chairs, and in front of the chairs were two pairs of nice warm slippers.

Elvira took off her wet coat and threw it down by the fireplace, *(kick feet)* kicked off her wet shoes, and then slipped her toes into a pair of the slippers.

Then she cried out, *"I'm in heeeeeere!"*

But still *(quietly again)* nobody said a word. Again she lifted her coffee cup and sipped slowly. When all of a sudden, she heard footsteps.

"Henry? Henry? *(call out loudly)* Is that you?"

The footsteps stopped behind her chair.

A voice said, *(very deep)* "Good eevening, madam."

Elvira said, *(eyes wide)* "Henry, that ain't you. *Is it?*"

And she turned slowly.

There standing behind Elvira was a very, very handsomely dressed gentleman in a black silk suit, long black leather boots, and a fancy frock tail coat.

There was only one thing wrong. *(one finger up)*

Hahaaaaaooooooooooooohhh!

"Henry? Henry? Is that you?"

No, of course it isn't. It's a very fine and handsomely dressed gentleman. And very polite, you know. The story is still building, and everything still seems quite normal except for one thing . . .

He didn't have a head. *(run finger across throat)*

Elvira said, "***Bwwaaaaa**aaaaaa! Who are you?*"

And the headless Haint spoke.

"Madam, so many years ago, I opened my home to two people *(pause)* just like you and your husband. I gave them hot food to eat and a nice warm place. But because I didn't show them where I hid my gold, they killed me. They *(finger cuts throat)* cut off my head.

"They buried my head in one part of the cellar, and my body in the other. I have kept this house alive and well, waiting for two nice people like you and your husband to help me get myself together again so that I can rest for eternity."

Elvira said, "Hoooo! But I don't know nothing about finding heads. I ain't never had to do that."

At that moment she heard Henry coming in.

"Oh," said Henry. "Finally found a place to put that old mule. *(gruff again)* Ooh, *(rub hands)* it's *cold*."

He stopped. "***Wooaaa!** (huge eyes)* Who is *that?*"

She said, "That's the man who owns this house."

Henry said, "Sure enough. How d'ya know this?"

Elvira said, "Henry, he told me."

"What did he tell you with? I don't see a mouth. I don't even see a head to hold a mouth."

Elvira said, "*Shhh!* He'll tell you."

And sure enough, the headless Haint told Henry the same story he told Elvira.

Henry said, "Well, sir. All due respect to you and your head and all, but to tell the truth, I ain't *never* had to find nobody's head."

"Sir," said the Haint, "do you see *(point)* that door?"

Henry looked and said, "Yeah, I do."

Nowadays, Haints and monsters can be pretty gruesome. But I didn't have that when I grew up. I heard my granddaddy's stories and that's what I chose from. I'd never heard of Frankenstein or Dracula, or anything like that. So my monsters are kind of quiet and bland, and closer to regular people. Like men with lots of hair and Haints without heads. And dogs, I have a lot of dog ghosts. But you know, a handsome man without a head is still scary, he really doesn't have to be slimy.

"If you go down the stairway behind that door, you will find a pick and a shovel," said the Haint. "If you dig beneath the cellar floor, you will find my head. Just help me get it back on my shoulders so I can rest for eternity."

Henry went over and opened the door.

Then he *(clap hands)* quickly slammed it shut.

"It's *daaaaark* down there," he said.

"Oh, I shall provide light for you," said the Haint.

He stepped to the fireplace and raised his hand into the air and placed a finger *(finger out)* in the flames. He lit the end of his finger, then removed the finger from his hand and handed it to Henry.

Henry said, *(hold finger, look both sides)* "Thank you."

He did the same with the other hand, removed the lit finger and handed the candle to Elvira.

"**Bwwwwaaaah!**" Elvira said. "Thank you."

Elvira and Henry took their candles down the stairs, found the pick and the shovels, and dug for the rest of the night. Just before the sun rose, they found the old Haint's head and *(lift both hands up)* placed it back on his shoulders.

As he adjusted himself once again into his head, he said to Elvira and Henry,

"I thank you both for helping me get myself together again. *Hahaaaaaaah.* As a reward, I want you to have this house and all the land.

"And if you will dig in back of the old oak tree in the backyard, you'll find my gold. It's yours."

And Elvira and Henry lived happily ever after.

. . . And *that's* the end of that.

"He lit the end of his finger . . ."

Well, I couldn't think of anywhere else to find a candle. Remember, I started writing this story way back in the fifth grade and I had a fifth grader's imagination. That's when you think of crazy stuff like that. Also, I let Elvira and Henry find the gold; Grandpa never did.

Many years after first writing the story, when I was all grown-up, I found it again and I told it at the National Storytelling Festival in Tennessee. The state tourism department liked it for some sort of state coming-home campaign. It made a lot of money for me, the story I started in the fifth grade.

THE HAIRY MAN

W iley was a little boy and he lived with his mama on the edge of the swamp. Every single day of little Wiley's life his mama would say, "Wiley, don't you ever, ever, *ever* go into that swamp by yourself."

And Wiley would say, "All right, Mama. I won't ever, ever, *ever* go into that swamp by myself."

And he would say, *(sweetly)* "*Why?*"

"Well, Wiley," she would say, "living way, way back inside that swamp is somebody known as *The Haaaaaairy Man*. He chases little children and when he catches them *(reach out)* *he eats them up*."

"*Oh*," Wiley said. "Well then, I ain't never going into that swamp by myself."

And Wiley's mother would pat his head and say, "You're a good boy, Wiley."

And Wiley would say, *(sweetly)* "I know."

One morning Wiley was in bed. Oh, it must have been 10:30 at least. Believe it was Saturday and Wiley didn't have to go to school. Or it could have been summer, he didn't have to go to school at all.

Whatever it was, he was asleep.

Wiley's Mama said, "*Wiiiileey!* Wiley, get up, son." Wiley sat up in bed, rubbed his eyes, and stretched.

"I'm up," he said.

She said, "Wiley, get up and wash your face. Put on your clothes and come downstairs, there's something I want you to see."

Wiley said, *(sweetly again)* "Okay."

"'WIIIILEEY! Wiley, get up, son' . . . 'I'm up,' he said."

BOOGIEMEN AND MONSTERS: *This is an old slave story that my grandpa told me when I was only three years old. Obviously it's a boogieman story, with that hairy man and all, but it starts quietly with a little boy who didn't have a dad, he just lived with his mom.*

She said, "You're a sweet boy, Wiley."

And Wiley said, "I know."

So Wiley put on his clothes and washed his face and went down the steps. There on the kitchen table were 50 jars of wild strawberry jam.

They were all hot. *Haaah!*

His mama had just finished pourin' 'em.

Wiley said, "I *love* strawberry jam."

"I know you do, Wiley," she said. "And I've made this special jar *(hold fingers up)* just for you."

And Wiley said, "I'm gonna eat it too. Hah."

So Wiley settled down and he ate every bit of his breakfast. He opened his jar of wild strawberry jam, took a spoon, and he ate *all* of that wild strawberry out of that one little jar. He *(lick, lick)* licked the spoon and he licked the jar and he ate the bread. *Haah!*

And Wiley said, "Mmmm. That was good."

His mama said, "I knew you would like that, son. Now, will you do your mama a favor?"

Wiley said, *(sweetly)* "Un *huh*."

She said, "Take this big jar of wild strawberry jam over to Granny's house." *(hold hand up)*

Wiley said, *(sweetly)* "Okay."

She said, "Now, Wiley, it doesn't take all day long to get to Granny's house. So you take that jar, but you come right back and clean up the backyard."

Wiley said, *(sweetly)* "Okay."

She said, "Wiley, you take a shortcut and come straight home. Take a shortcut through the swamp."

And Wiley said, *(shake head slowly)* "Uh uh."

"Wiley? What did you say?"

"I said, *(shake head no)* uh uh."

"I LOVE strawberry jam."

▬▬▬▬▬▬▬▬

Mm. I loved hot wild strawberry jam too 'cause it was kind of tart. Granny could never get it sweet enough. It always had that little sting that hit me in the side of my jaw. I loved that. So naturally, wild strawberry jam somehow finds its way into my stories a lot.

"Wiley, I'm your mama. What are you sayin'?"

And Wiley said to her, "Well, I'm your little boy, and I'm sayin', *Uh uh*."

"Wiley, why are you saying that to me?"

Wiley said, "Well, Mama, all my life you told me that the Hairy Man lives in the swamp and that he'd chase me and he'd catch me and he'd eat me up.

"Now you're sending me into the swamp. Do you *want* him to chase me and catch me and eat me up?"

"Son," she said. "I told you that when you were a little, little boy. I didn't want you disappearing into that swamp. Now you are a *big* little boy. You can go in that swamp and come out that swamp. Nobody will bother you if you do *exactly* what I say."

Wiley said, "Mama, *(frown)* you better tell me *exactly* what I should do."

"Nobody will bother you . . ."

She said, "Good. Come this way."

She took Wiley over to the sink and showed him a shelf. There on the shelf was a glass of milk.

She said, "Wiley, do you see this glass of milk?"

And Wiley said, "Uh huh."

She said, "Wiley, it's *magic*."

And Wiley said, "Ha?"

She said, "Wiley, if you should go in the swamp, and the Hairy Man should get to chasing you, this *(point)* glass of milk will tell me. It will turn red. I will know for sure that the Hairy Man is after you."

Wiley said, "Wonderful. *Aaah*, but whatcha gonna do after the glass of milk turns red, *hah?*"

She said, "After that I'm gonna go to the barn, I'm gonna *(three hand motions)* untie your three hound dogs and send them into the swamp to protect you. The Hairy Man is *scared* of hound dogs."

"Mama, *hmmm*, you don't have to do that. You don't have to do *that*."

And she said, "Whatever do you mean, son?"

"You don't have to send them dogs after me," he said, "'cause you see, Mama, when I leave here them dogs are leaving with me."

"Wiley, them dogs are playful. They'll chase all kinds of critters, birds, rabbits, snakes, and squirrels. They'll be off somewhere chasing some critter and won't even *know* the Hairy Man is chasing you. Leave them tied up. If the glass of milk turns red, I'll untie 'em and *(point)* send them straight after you."

So Wiley said, "Let's go find them dogs."

They went outside and they found all three of Wiley's hound dogs, and they tied each of them

Ah, so we have a hairy monster and we add something else that's magic. Again, I am building my story triangle, setting the scene, describing all the details that the story will need to work. A magic glass of milk? Well, Wiley is still cautious, but he trusts his mama. And where would the story go if Wiley took his hound dogs along?

Even when telling a story which is not all that gruesome or scary, it's always good to remember a child can look at you as if to say, "I don't understand that." Maybe that's not the day for that kind of tale. Don't be afraid to stop, feel at home enough to say, "Maybe that story is not a good one for today, I'll tell you a different one." Read your audience just as I do.

on a piece of rope. Then Mama handed Wiley
that great big jar of wild strawberry jam.

Wiley said goodbye to his mama. He went out
the back door, across the porch, down the steps,
across the walk, across the road, and into the swamp.

As Wiley walked along, he happened to look up
in the trees, and hangin' down was long green snakes,
(snaky motions) watching Wiley as he walked along.

Further down in the swamp, where the limbs
of the trees grew close to the ground, you could see
great big old birds (big eyes) watching Wiley walk along.

Further down in the swamp you could hear
a *splish* and a *splash*, and that was an old alligator
crawling into the muddy waters of the swamp.

But Wiley wasn't afraid of the alligators.

Wiley was not afraid of those great big old birds.

"... he happened to look up ..."

**Yes, it was daaaark in there, with
slimy green things hanging from
the trees and big old birds. But
Wiley, he wasn't scared of them,
he was scared of something he'd
never seen, something that was
made of nothing but pure hair ...**

Wiley wasn't even afraid of them green snakes hanging out of the trees. What Wiley was afraid of was comin' up behind him.

All at once he heard, *(real deep voice)*

"***Helloooooo** there, Wiley.*"

And Wiley said, *(eyes very wide)* "*Uh* oh."

But all Wiley could do was say, *(real quiet)*

"How do you do, *(wave)* Mister Hairy Man?"

There standing behind him was *The Haairy Man.*

The Hairy Man said, *(very deep)* "***Heheeeeeeee!***

Hello there, Wiley. Haaaaah! How ya doin'?"

And Wiley said, *(sweetly)* "Not so good."

"***Welllll***, Wiley," said The Hairy Man. *(sly smile)*

"I'm glad to see you, boy. You know what?

Every day I goes down to your backyard there, and I looks over, and I sees you playin' ball.

"HELLOOOOOOOO there, Wiley."

Sometimes a monster becomes a real favorite. My niece Ava, she just loves the Hairy Man, she's looking for him all over. When we traveled to New Orleans once, Ava sat up the whole night by the window with the curtain up. She was looking for the Hairy Man, she had to see him. I'm laying there with my gowns on and she keeps going, "There he is! There he is!" That girl was something. So I said, "We'll go to the swamp, we'll see the Hairy Man there."

"And I says to myself, I says, *Look at Wiley!* Heheeeeeee, he's playin' ball. Haaaaah. Maybe he'll come into the swamp, I says to myself, and he'll play with me. And here you are, Wiley, here you are.

"I'm glad to have you here, Wiley."

And Wiley said, *(sweetly)* "Thank you."

"Wiley, what is that you got in your hand boy, ha? What is that? *(point)* What is that, Wiley?"

Wiley was so scared, he was shakin' so hard, he could barely say,

"W-w-well, Mister Hairy Man, this here's *(hands up)* a jar of wild strawberry jam that my mama made. That's what it is. I'm takin' it to Granny's house."

And the Hairy Man said, "*Whoaaa!* I love strawberry jam, I *love* it. Specially when it's *wild*.

"Well, tell you what I'm gonna do, Wiley. Tell you what I'm gonna do. I'm gonna eat that jar of wild strawberry jam here, I'm gonna eat it up, I'm gonna eat it all. *Haah!* And when I get through eating that jar of wild strawberry jam, *haaaaaaaa*, then *(clap hands)* I'm gonna eat you too."

And Wiley said, *(real scared)* "Uh *oh*."

And he took that jar of wild strawberry jam, set it down on the ground, and started running.

Now, Wiley had real short little legs, but they could go *real* fast. *(fingers run)* He was pickin' 'em up and puttin' 'em down. Oh, that little boy was running as fast as his legs could carry him. Over the trees, under the trees, around the trees, through the trees. He was runnin' and runnin' and runnin'. *(run, run fingers)*

And that Hairy Man, he was lopin' along behind.

"And Wiley said, 'Uh OH.'"

Now, you know, I don't describe the Hairy Man at all, I don't say if he has a head or a mouth or eyes or anything. It's better to let the scene create the characters, and give the children's imagination a chance to invent how they look.

You could hear that Hairy Man sayin', *(panting)*
"Whooooossh, look at them little legs run."
But it didn't do Wiley a bit of good.
His little ol' legs, they just kept on runnin', but that ol' Hairy Man ran right up behind him,
grabbed that little boy by his T-shirt, *(grab and raise up)*
lifted him high up into the air,
threw his hairy head back, and *(mouth wide)*
opened his mouth.
Wiley's little ol' legs, well, they were still runnin' when they got up in the air. That ol' Hairy Man was opening his mouth, gettin' ready to drop that little boy down his throat . . . *(big pause)*
In the meantime, back at home, Wiley's mama had been out in the apple orchard. She had picked a bucket of apples and poured 'em in a sink of water.

". . . look at them little legs run."

The boogieman is lifting Wiley way up, throwing his head back, and opening his mouth. Wiley's legs still churn around, even off the ground, not giving up. A real clear picture of disaster, but in the meantime, back at home . . .

And she was *(wash hands)* washing them apples.
She was going to make her little boy somethin' good.

He just loved apples. *(still washing)*

She wasn't sure what she was gonna make him, but he was gonna enjoy it. She picked up an apple and a knife. She was peelin' that apple and thinkin' about what she was gonna make for her little boy.

"I ought to make him an apple pie," she thought. "Yaah, he'd like an apple pie with some brown sugar, with a little butter in it. Oh yeah, Wiley'd love that."

As she was peelin' that apple, she just happened to look up on the shelf behind the sink.

The glass of milk had turned red.

Mama knew the Hairy Man was chasin' her boy.

She threw that apple one way, *(throw left)*
threw that knife the other way, *(throw right)*
ran out the back door and down the steps,
across the yard and into the barn.

Then she untied all three of Wiley's hound dogs and said to the hound dogs, "Go into the swamp and rescue Wiley. *The Hairy Man's done caught him.*"

And the hound dogs, they looked at her, and they looked at each other, and they said,

"*Whooofhooof! Rowooowf! Rowoofwoof!*"

Now, you know, that's hound dog language for *Wiley's in trouble. Let's go and get him.*

You have never, never heard the kind of noise that them hound dogs made going across that field. Across the field and over into the swamp, they was barkin' and howlin' and carryin' on.

Back in the swamp, the Hairy Man *(grip hand up again)* was getting ready to gulp that little boy right down

"Whooofhooof! Rowooowf!..."

The magic milk has worked! All three of them hound dogs take off to rescue Wiley. Everything in the story has reached the top of the story triangle, everything is going to come together at once.

his throat when he stopped. He heard something.

He listened.

He said, "Wiley, did you just hear somethin'?"

And Wiley said, *(sweetly)* "Uh *huh*."

"What did you hear?"

"I heard my hound dogs."

"Wiley, do you know I'm scared of hound dogs?"

"Uh huh," Wiley said. "I know you are."

"Wiley, which way are them hound dogs comin'?"

"They's comin' this way," Wiley said.

"Wiley, if them hound dogs are comin' this way, then I oughtta go *that* way."

Wiley said, *(nod sweetly)* "Go right ahead."

The Hairy Man threw Wiley down on the ground, and he started runnin'. But the *moment* he lifted one foot to run, the hound dogs got him.

"*Whooofhooof! Rowooowf! Rowoofwoof!*"

Tore him limb from limb. *Haah!*

Nothing left of the Hairy Man.

As for Wiley, he went and grabbed that big jar of wild strawberry jam, took it to Granny's house, and come back right through the swamp.

And *(nod sweetly)* he cleaned up the backyard.

That night after supper, Wiley and his mama each had a wedge of that apple pie with a little bit of homemade ice cream on top.

And now Wiley goes in and out of that swamp, and *nobody*,

specially that Hairy Man,

ever bothers him.

. . . And *that's* the end of that.

"Wiley, did you just hear . . ."

Oh, I love these little dialogues you can make up. You remember that the Hairy Man wanted Wiley to come to the swamp and play with him. He seems to like Wiley even though he plans to eat him. This hairy monster has a funny soft spot, and I think that's why my niece Ava likes him so much.

It was the time of year they call Indian Summer. It had been a hot day. The old woman was tired from the few chores that she still tried to do at home. She opened the screen door and stood there for a while. Then she walked onto the porch and settled herself down into a chair.

She took a great big deep breath and turned her face toward the highway. She sort of chuckled.

"The traffic goes on and on.

"Where do the people go? Mmm, they just move."

The cars never stopped. Her house was the only house on the road, so if they turned, they would come in to visit. But no one ever visited.

Except maybe Honeyboy.

Any time she thought about her son Honeyboy, a smile bent her face. And she thought about all the wonderful things that her son had done for her.

Even when he was a little boy.

He would find a pretty feather, or rock, *(gentle smile)* or a flower, and he'd always bring it back to her.

Now he was a grown man, and he never missed a birthday or Christmas or any holiday.

But Honeyboy just wouldn't stay.

Was it that she had not known what to do with the child? After his father had passed away so soon after his birth, what had happened? Why was it that she couldn't do anything for her child?

She turned once again to look out to the highway. And just at that moment a car turned off the road.

"Honeyboy just wouldn't stay."

QUIET AND SUBTLE STORIES: *Now, this is a very different kind of tale. Not much happens and the clues are very subtle, so the listener must pay attention while the characters play the drama. It takes place in the thirties, and nearly everything was different. People were different, and even our criminology was different. Perhaps you'll understand what I mean when you read the story.*

She looked at the car and saw she had a visitor.

She placed the strands of hair behind her head, patted the bun at her neck, straightened her apron, squared her shoulders, and prepared for a guest.

The car pulled before the gate.

And her eyes, those 76-year-old eyes, they didn't see so good anymore, but she heard the footfalls. It was a heavy person. She heard the gate squeak and now she could see who it was.

"Well, Lords it be. Sheriff, what you doin' here? Come up and set a spell."

The Sheriff stood before her, removed his hat, and *(hand under arm)* he placed it beneath his arm.

"Sheriff, what you doin' here?"

Again, you really must be able to see, to visualize your stories. You can help listeners understand the characters by playing every part as if you were the character. This great big old sheriff is heavy and kinda dumb. I see that and I feel that. His stomach hangs out and he lumbers around like a heavy football. But the woman is the opposite, she's small and gentle.

"No, ma'am," the Sheriff said. *(serious)* "I can't stay. I've come out here on business."

"Oh, Sheriff, what kind of business you got with an old woman like me? *(little smile)* What have I done?"

"No, ma'am," he said. "You ain't done nothin'. I just need to talk to ya."

"Well, Sheriff, ain't no need to stand up there, it's too hot. Come on over here and sit down."

"Yes, ma'am, I just need to ask you this."

"All right, all right, what is it?"

"Miss Jesse, um. When have you seen your son?"

"When have I seen Honeyboy?"

"Yes, ma'am."

"Well now, let's see. *(softly)* Oh yes, I almost forgot. Honeyboy come here last week. It was my birthday, and he brought me my present."

"Last week. Now, what day was that?"

"I believe it was Wednesday."

"You ain't seen him since?"

"No, Sheriff, he ain't been here. What's wrong?"

"Miss Jesse, I just don't know how to tell you this. But you see, they brought a body into my office

"You ain't seen him since?"

But the Sheriff looks serious, he's all business. These little details do more to give the right feeling of a story than you think when you're telling it. You don't really register them, but your listeners do. All of a sudden you have a clear scene, a Sheriff with his big belts standing over a frail woman in a rocking chair. Both are being polite in a very difficult situation.

last night," the Sheriff said. *(pause)* "It was Honeyboy.

"But you know, I can't be *sure* it was Honeyboy."

"Now, Sheriff, wait ... What're you sayin' to me? You can't be sure it was Honeyboy? But Honeyboy and your children played together all their lives. You know what my Honeyboy looks like. What do you mean you can't be sure it's Honeyboy?"

"No, ma'am, I don't mean that. I mean, this man was shot at close range in the back of the head, and when the bullet come through . . . well, we just can't tell who it is. The only thing that reminds me of Honeyboy is that scar, that birthmark, you know, that one on his shoulder that looks like a beehive. Ain't that why you named your boy Honeyboy?"

"Yes, sir. *(small voice)* Is that all?"

"Yes, ma'am," he said. "I need you to come down and identify the body."

"Sheriff, I don't think that's my boy," she said. "Seems to me like I would know he was dead. I don't have no feeling that my boy is dead. I know what you all been sayin', I know I got a bad boy, I know Honeyboy's bad. I read the papers and seen how he robbed, and they say he killed and shot folks.

"But sometimes it just ain't true," she said. "I hear on the radio that he's done robbed somebody over in Genoa City, and then two hours later, he's 700 miles away and he's killing somebody else.

"So you see, I don't believe that's the truth."

"Miss Jesse, I didn't come to bad-mouth your boy. I know Honeyboy helps, I know he helps folks. But you see, that boy's got a reward on his head. *DEAD OR ALIVE*, it says, *5,000 dollars*. You know, folks is gonna be gunning for him."

"Sheriff, did somebody kill him you know of?"

"Oh, Miss Jesse, I knew you would ask me that. Yes, ma'am, somebody killed him that I know of."

"Well, who was it?"

The Sheriff thought for a long time, and then he looked the old woman straight in the eye and said,

"James Franklin."

The old woman laughed at him.

"I know Honeyboy helps . . ."

Yes, even crime was different in the thirties. Honeyboy robbed and stole, but he left money and food on people's porches. It was crime, but it was help that people needed too. Honeyboy is both bad and generous, which makes what happens to him interesting.

"*Hah.* Sheriff, *James Franklin* was Honeyboy's best friend. They slept in the same bed, they drank out of the same glass, ate out of the same plate. They was good friends all of their lives.

"Now, James comes over here and cuts my wood and brings it in, he takes care of me, and he's always askin' for Honeyboy. Ain't nobody *that* low-down."

"Miss Jesse, you don't understand. When you got a reward on your head of 5,000 dollars dead or alive, you ain't got no good friends."

"Sheriff, you want me to identify that body?"

"Yes, ma'am."

"Well, let me fix myself up and I'll go with you."

"Ain't nobody THAT low-down."

"It can't be my boy, not killed by his best friend, not for money." But notice she understands that James always asks for Honeyboy, that he likes to know where he is. That's subtle, but it's important. Another clue that helps build the story is "a fine piece of uptown furniture." I think of walnut wood when I say that, I want you to think about it like the sheriff did.

Miss Jesse walked in the house. In her bedroom, she removed her apron, placed her hat on her head, and threw a coat over her shoulders.

The Sheriff stood looking around the living room. His gaze fell on a radio. He walked over to it.

"Miss Jesse, this here is a mighty fine piece of uptown furniture you got. Where did you get it?"

"That was my birthday present from Honeyboy."

"Yes, ma'am, it's nice," he said. "Are you ready?"

They drove in silence to town.

Finally the Sheriff turned down the main street. The old lady leaned up in her seat and she said,

"Sheriff, how come all them people are standing at the furniture store? What're they wantin'?"

He said, "Ma'am, you know how people are, they're just curious. And you know that Honeyboy helped a whole lot of them folks. They want to know if it's Honeyboy that's layin' a corpse in there."

The Sheriff stopped the car, walked around and opened the door, and helped the old lady out. As she walked through the crowd, one man after the other stepped back and removed his hat.

"Mr. Henry, don't you worry . . ."

As I tell this story, I can see the strength of the old woman as she greets old friends and she calms them as she walks into the store. In those old days, furniture and cabinet makers were the coffin makers, and the town undertaker was often a furniture salesman.

And Miss Jesse would walk up to them and say,

"Mr. Henry, don't you worry, that ain't Honeyboy.

"Willie, how you doin'? Hear y'got a set of twins. You take care of them babies, ha*haaa*.

"You dry you eyes, that ain't Honeyboy."

One to the other, she assured them Honeyboy wasn't the corpse that lay inside the furniture store. One after the other, until she stood at the door.

And there in front of her was James Franklin.

"Well," she said. "Here's my boy James Franklin. James, somebody told me your mama's been ailing."

James said, "Y-yes, ma'am, she ain't feelin' good."

"Well, James, now you listen. You come over and cut some wood tomorrow, and I'll make your mama some chicken and dumplings, she always likes my chicken and dumplings. Don't you forget now."

He said, *(look down)* "Yes, ma'am."

And he stepped back, not sure what to say or do. The Sheriff opened the door.

Two Deputy Sheriffs bowed their heads, removed their hats, and walked in front of the old woman.

There stood a gurney, with a white sheet across it. The Sheriff took his bulk around the other side.

"Miss Jesse," he said, *(uneasy)* "I sure enough hate to ask you to do this. I done seen it, and this here is horrible. It's horrible to look at."

Miss Jesse said, "Now, Sheriff, come sit down. I'm an old woman, I done seen many horrible things in my life. One more ain't gonna hurt me."

She said, "Now, tell me what you want me to do."

He said, "Well, ma'am, I'm gonna pull the sheet off for you. I want you to look at this body, and I want you to tell me if you recognize who it is."

"Sheriff, *(quietly)* I can move the sheet myself."

She picked up the end of the sheet, still watching the Sheriff. She pulled it slowly back over the body. And then *(hesitate)* she looked down at the body.

Never changed the expression on her face.

She leaned over and she looked at the birthmark. She looked at the face that was no longer there. And she looked at what she could see of the body.

"I can move the sheet myself."

I told this story for three years before I could see the old woman clearly. She was never black; at first she was just small and pale. Then I was sitting in a shopping mall in Nebraska, and there was an awful storm outside; we were told to move away from the glass so that the people could come in from the parking lot. The doors opened and in came this little woman with a shopping bag; her glasses were wet and her hair was all over her head. Then she stood there against the glass, grabbing at her coat and wiping off her glasses, but she just made them worse. So finally she took them off, pushed her hair back on her head, and wiped her face. "Oh my God, that's Honeyboy's mama," I said. And that is what I see every time I tell this story.

Once again, she lifted both hands, took the sheet, and *(lift trembling hands)* pulled it back across the body.

Had you been watching her, you could just barely see the right hand begin to shake uncontrollably.

She stood back.

And she said to the Sheriff, "That ain't my boy. That ain't my boy." *(slowly shake head)*

The Sheriff said, "Ma'am, did you look at him? Did you take a good look? See the birthmark? Can't you tell me? Can't you tell me for sure?"

"Sheriff, a mama knows her child. I don't know who this is. But *(low voice)* it ain't my child."

"Miss Jesse . . . All right, all right, ma'am."

"Had you been watching her . . ."

Oh, Honeyboy, I do love to do this story. It's a thinking story, but you gotta listen hard. You have to see that Miss Jesse. She gave herself away when she began to shake, probably right when she saw that birthmark. She really didn't know if it was gonna be her son, but she wanted to move that sheet herself. If the Sheriff had done it, she would not have had control, she had to be in control.

And then the Sheriff turned to the Deputies.

"Arrest . . . James Franklin for murder," he said.

The Deputies put their hats back on their heads, bowed politely to Miss Jesse, and left the room.

Miss Jesse turned slowly to the door.

The Sheriff placed his hand beneath her arm when she staggered just a bit, and they walked slowly toward the door. You could hear outside,

"Noooooo! Go back! Tell her to look again!

"*She knows* it's Honeyboy," James Franklin said. "She *knows* it's him. That's my best friend. I know Honeyboy, *that's him.* Dead or alive, it said. I killed my best friend and *you owe me 5,000 dollars.*"

The screen door opened slowly and Miss Jesse walked to the edge of the steps.

James Franklin stood up.

She walked toward him and she whispered,

"Don't you forget now, James, *(quiet smile)* your mama needs some chicken and dumplings. You come out and cut that wood for me."

And she turned away and walked to the car.

The men pulled their hats from their heads,

"I killed my best friend . . ."

Poor James Franklin, he thought Honeyboy's mama was stupid. You see, back in those days, the body had to be identified before a reward was given. If it wasn't, nobody got credit and nobody got the money. If the next of kin said, "That's not Honeyboy," as Miss Jesse said, then that body was not Honeyboy. No reward. James Franklin was going to jail.

took huge gray handkerchiefs from their pockets, and they wiped their faces.

She got into the car, looking only straight ahead. The Sheriff turned the car away from curb and he drove out of town. As they drove along she said,

"Sheriff, can I ask you something?"

"Yes, ma'am, Miss Jesse. What is it?"

"When somebody ain't got family like that boy, ain't got nobody at all, how do you bury them?"

"Oh, Miss Jesse, now, don't you worry about that. You see, we got us a potter's field, and the county pays for the burial."

"Oh, Sheriff, that's good. You know, I think all human beings should be buried decently."

He said, "Yes, ma'am."

He stopped the car at her gate and he started to get out, but she touched his arm.

"It's all right, Sheriff," she said. "I've been goin' in and out of this house some 60 years, I can make it. I just want to say I'm sorry I couldn't help you."

"Oh, Miss Jesse, don't you worry, you done good, real good. I'm sorry I had to put you through that."

She said, "I'll be all right, you just go on."

He said, "Now, are you sure?"

"Oh yes, Sheriff, I'm all right."

She got out, and she leaned over and she waved. As the Sheriff backed the car out, she stood there, watching as the dust went into swirls and settled on the other side of the road, onto the leaves.

Nobody could see the tears as they met down beneath her chin and dropped to her blouse.

She turned around. Blinded by her tears, she fumbled the gate open. Stumbling from one side of the walkway to the other, she finally got to the stoop.

She walked up the steps, pushed the door open, and walked across the room to touch the radio.

All she could say was, *"Honeyboy, Honeyboy.*

"That's all I could do for you, son.

"That's all I could do for you."

... And *that's* the end of that.

"Nobody could see the tears ..."

_____

Well, you see, Honeyboy's mama lost her son and he was all she had, but she fixed it. She had to give him up, but she made sure his killer was put away for good.

Many, many years ago and far, far away lived a man and his wife and their son. The man was old, and the woman was quite old, but the son was very young. And that was a good thing. Had it not been for this young man, the man and the woman could not live, for they were too old to work.

The young man worked in a sawmill, using a *huuuge* (arms very wide) band saw.

Every day he got up from his bed and walked to the mill in the town. Every night he came home tired and exhausted, (eyes closed) begging his father,

"Please, I *must* stay home to rest.

"I cannot breathe another day in that mill."

But the old man said, "Son, look at your mother. She is an old woman, and I must care for her. And I am an old man, and you must care for me.

"One day, my boy, one day there will be a miracle. One day you will come home and rest and get well, and you won't need to work again."

But every day, once again, the young man would get up and go to his work in the mill.

Well, (pause, look up) it was a late stormy night. The old man sat gazing into the fireplace, and the old woman sat sipping her tea, watching her son lay before her feet (spread arms low) in the warmth of the fire.

"There is a storm raging," the old man said.

"My friend cannot get here tonight."

". . . it was a late stormy night."

ABOUT FEAR AND GHOSTS: *Oh boy, ghosts are just out-and-out interesting. They got the best stories. If you unwind the story just right, especially a good classic story like this one, you can cause goose bumps that wear clothes. That kind of fear is wonderful, and as I say, it's one of our human emotions that is not exercised enough. You make love, you laugh, your funny bone is tickled all the time, you satisfy all the other feelings you have, but you don't get scared enough. So when an opportunity presents itself, you should hang right in there and let your fear happen.*

"Oh," said the old woman. "The Sergeant Major is a *strong* old man. He shall be here."

"I miss him so much," said the old man. "And we have aged. The winds may blow too strong for him to walk up that hill."

With that *(look up)* there was a knock upon the door.

The old woman placed her finger at her lips, opened the door, and there was the Sergeant Major.

"*Well, woman?* *(gruff)* *Let me in!* I am *cold.*"

"Oh, please," she said. "Come in, come in."

She removed his coat, and the old man beckoned to his friend. "Come here, sit down here beside me, and get yourself warm," he said.

"*Ooh,*" the Sergeant Major said. *(rub hands)* "It's *cold* out there. I almost didn't make it up that hill."

"I was worried, my friend," the old man said. "I'm glad to see you. Do you have your pipe?"

"*Aaah,*" the Sergeant Major said, "I'm always with my pipe. But I don't have any tobacco. I very seldom smoke anymore," he said.

The old man reached down and lifted his pouch. "My son, your godson, he buys my tobacco. I'm sure he would not mind if you helped me smoke it."

"Oh," said the Sergeant Major. "*Wonderful.*" He reached into his pocket for his pipe. As he pulled it out, something fell to the floor. He looked around, scooped it up, and placed it back in his pocket.

Then he filled his pipe with tobacco and lit it.

The man said, "What was *that?* What *was* that? That fell to the floor? *(point down)* I saw it."

"Oh," said the Sergeant Major. "It's just a trinket that I carry. A trinket that I acquired in India.

"It's just a trinket that I carry."

▬▬▬▬▬▬▬▬▬▬▬▬▬

As I tell these stories, I must say I don't know whether I believe in ghosts or not. I do know of times when I've run into what I thought was a ghost. Still, I can't really believe in that stuff because I've read too much about what your mind can do to itself, what it can create on its own. Our minds haven't been met deep enough, I think, to always know what's real and what isn't. Like the time I physically saw my grandmother when I walked out in front of three thousand people at Purdue University. It was one of the first big audiences I had, I didn't know what to do, and I thought, "I don't have any business out here. If I'm going to quit, now is the time to do it." I turned to go back and there stood Grandma, her hand on her hip, looking at me. "Now, where d'you think you're going?"

"Nothing that you should worry about," he said.

"But," the old man said, "we are good friends. Why are you *hiding* things from me?"

And the Sergeant Major said, "I'm not *hiding* anything, man. But it's . . . it's something that I don't think you want to know about."

He pulled it out, held it to the light of the fire, and *(turn hand)* turned it first one way, then the other.

The old man said, "My *God*, man! What is *that?*"

And the Sergeant Major said,

"It's called . . . *the Monkey's Paw*. It's *magic*.

"If you own it, you will want to throw it away. It's an *evil* thing. It contains three wishes. If you make the first wish, you must make the other two."

"Oh," said the old man. "Oh, such *foolery*."

The Sergeant Major said, "You hold the paw up,

"My GOD, man! What is THAT?"

At first people are sure they know this story and they think, "Oh no, I have to sit through that again?" But later they come and say, "I've never heard it like that before." I really think it's the way I play the characters, the way I become the story and bring these people into it. One said he had never been so frightened before as an adult. Sitting watching me, he knows the story the whole time, and still he's wiping down the chill bumps.

and make a wish. If it *moves*, your wish comes true.

"I have tried to *(thrust hand out)* *throw* it away,

"I have tried to *give* it away," he said.

"I have tried to *DESTROY* it."

And with that he threw the paw into the fire.
They sat and watched, but nothing happened to it.
The old man stood and raked it from the fireplace.

"It does not burn! *It does not burn!*" he said.

"Leave it there, man," said the Sergeant Major.
"Leave it there!" But the old man lifted it up.

"Does it really work? Does it *really work?*"

"Oh, you own it now," the Sergeant Major said.
"You touched it. Throw it back into the fire, it's *evil!*
I'm telling you, *IT'S EVIL!*" he said.

"Yes, I shall remember that," the old man said.
And he placed it in his pocket.

They talked of many things that night. As the Sergeant Major was dressing to leave, he said again,

"Throw it back into the fire.

"*Throw it away!* *(whisper)* *Throw it AWAY!*"

"I shall remember," the old man said.

The door closed.

The young man rose to his knees and said,

"*Is this it, Father?* Is this the miracle we have been waiting for so long? Can we wish for money? Can I come home and get well?"

"Did you not hear your godfather? It's *evil*."

"Father, please. If we wish for a small amount of money, perhaps the evil will not be so great."

The old man was frightened.

But he saw what was in his child's eyes. The need to rest. He removed the paw from his pocket.

"Perhaps," he said, "if we wish for a small amount of money, the evil will not be so great."

"I . . . wish," the old man said. *(eyes closed, raise hand)*

"I wish for two . . . hundred . . . pounds."

He watched the paw . . . *and it moved. (jump back)*

And he threw it to the floor. *(cast hand down)*

The next morning the young man once again went to work. Late in the evening, as the old woman prepared the tea, awaiting her son's arrival at home, there was a knock at the door. The old man said,

"My son knocks?"

And he opened the door. Standing there was a finely dressed young man from town. He removed his hat and placed it beneath his arm.

"'I . . . wish,' the old man said."

The old man was frightened, but his fear wasn't great enough to resist his son, and that's going to get him in trouble. That's a good message for children. In the old story of "Little Red Riding Hood," the wolf didn't tie Granny in the closet, you know. Oh no, the wolf ate Granny up. Then he ate two of the little pigs too. But children don't hear the old version today, the one telling you that if you get off the path, the wolf will eat you up. Yes, he will. Scary tales are actually cautions. Hans Christian Anderson told us that, and so did those frightening tales written by the Grimm Brothers. They knew you had to scare children so that they will be careful. All children must have some fear, they must learn all about caution very early.

I believe that if you tell children frightening things, but help them know the security of their mother and father, their teachers and all the people who love them, then you don't have to worry. I believe that scary tales teach them this. If they don't hear about frights, they will discover them later in life, and that may not be so good.

"Sir, I bring you news from the mill."

"Yes," said the old man. "Come in. *Come in.* My son is due at any time."

"*Sir*, there's been an accident. *It-it was your son. W-we tried* to warn him. We watched him walk into the saw. Well, *(anguish)* *he's dead.*

"We couldn't stop him. We tried, *but he's dead.*"

The old man said, "*Noooo!*"

And the old woman said, "*My child?*"

The young man said, "We cannot be responsible for the accident. But we have taken a small purse to help you bury him. Here is two hundred pounds."

The next day there was a service. And a burial.

The old man and the old woman returned home.

"My child," the woman said, "the paw has taken my child. Make it *(despairing)* *bring . . . him . . . BACK!*"

"The old man said, 'NOOOO!'"

The man said, "Do you know what you're *asking?* Do you not *understand* what happened to him?"

"I understand," the woman said. "But there are two more wishes in the paw. It took my child away, now make it *bring . . . him . . . BACK* from the grave."

And the old man said, "I am frightened."

But he removed the paw from his pocket, and he held it to the light and he said, (trembling)

"Bring . . . my . . . child . . . back!

"Bring him back from the grave, *bring him back!"*

And the paw *moved.* He threw it to the floor.

They waited and listened. Long past midnight, the candles burned low and then out.

After a while they heard,

Squuuueeeeeeeeeeeeeeeeeerrrrrrrrrrrrk.

"After a while they heard, Squuuueeeeeeeeeeeerrrrrrrrrrk."

The old woman turned to the old man and said, "That's the door, *that's the door! He's come back!*"

Squuuueeeeeeeeeeeeeeeeerrrrrrrrrrrrk.

"Open the door," she said. *"Open the door!"*

The old man said, *"Nooo! Don't you understand?* Don't you *understand* what you will *see?*"

"Yes," she said. "I will see my child."

And she stood up and walked toward the door. But there were many locks on the door, for you see, there were many highwaymen upon the roads.

She started to pull the locks, one by one. As she lifted the last lock and reached for the doorknob,

"No, *nooooo!*" the old man said. *(hold head)*

Suddenly he remembered he had one last wish.

He fell to his knees searching for the paw.

The old woman grabbed the doorknob, and as she turned it, the old man found the paw, lifted it up into the air, and screamed,

"Go away, go AWAY! Go BACK into the grave!"

The woman opened the door. *(jump back)*

But there was nobody. *There was nobody there.*

But *(quietly)* the gate . . .

The gate at the end of the walk was *moving* . . . as if someone or some*thing* had just passed through.

I must warn you. *(lean forward)*

If at any time you should place your hand deep into your pocket and feel something strange . . .

(loud) Throw it away!

(very loud) THROW IT AWAY!

It might just be . . . *The Monkey's Paw.* *(eyes very wide)*

. . . And *that's* the end of *that.*

"THROW IT AWAY!"

You know, I tell lots of scary tales about ghosts, and some of them have been documented. Truth can be stranger than fiction, and some strange things have really happened. "The Monkey's Paw" isn't one of them, of course, but that doesn't mean I can't give it a good bloodcurdling scream at the end. People have jumped up right out of their seats. Once, a high school coach fell back and wedged himself in a trash can. That was good, yes, I liked that.